Regional Resurgence in Africa: Prospects and Challenges of African Union

Regional Resurgence in Africa: Prospects and Challenges of African Union

Sandipani Dash

Vij Books India Pvt Ltd
New Delhi (India)

Indian Council of World Affairs
Sapru House, New Delhi

Published by

Vij Books India Pvt Ltd
(Publishers, Distributors & Importers)
2/19, Ansari Road
Delhi – 110 002
Phones: 91-11-43596460, 91-11-47340674
Fax: 91-11-47340674
e-mail: vijbooks@rediffmail.com
web : www.vijbooks.com

ISBN: 978-93-85563-74-4 (Hardback)

ISBN: 978-93-85563-75-1 (ebook)

Contents

Preface

The regional identity formation is underpinned by a process that involves a group of states and people identifying a set of common problems linked to their geographic space and finding solutions to these problems somewhere in between individual state initiative and the larger global intervention. The regional community's assertion of its own identity is, many a time, perceived as a response to the categorization it is historically subjected to by the extra-regional powers which are entrenched in the region.

Regional resurgence in Africa is a process of self-construction of identity and its institutional manifestation is reflected in the African Union's (AU) evolution based on the premise of 'African solution to the African problem.' A continent wide grouping of as many as 54 member states, the regional institution has completed fifty years of its existence, with formation of the Organisation of African Unity (OAU) in 1963 and its reformation into the AU in 2002, demonstrating phenomenal resilience and resurgence.

Celebrating the 50th Anniversary of the OAU-AU, African leaders declared 2013 to be the year of *Pan-Africanism and African Renaissance* in order to provide an opportunity to reflect on its past, re-kindle its ideals and plan for better future of Africa and its people. They agreed upon a strategic framework *Agenda 2063* envisaging socio-economic transformation of the continent over the next 50 years. It builds on, and seeks to accelerate the implementation of past and existing continental initiatives developed at national, regional and continental levels to ensure growth and sustainable development.

The transition from the OAU to the AU is based on the ideational shift from 'secretive' sovereignty to 'collective' sovereignty. The AU has consequently institutionalized African Peace and Security Architecture (APSA) and African Governance Architecture (AGA). While APSA concerns peace and security matter of the continent, AGA is the overall political and institutional framework for the promotion of good governance in Africa. Given the exclusive emphasis put on the APSA, there is now a realization for creating synergies between the AGA and the APSA.

A careful scrutiny of the existing literature on the AU indicates that any holistic academic exercise of the subject is a rarity. The research project has tried to fill this analytical gap, by looking at the issue of Pan-African Regionalism from a comprehensive security perspective. It has also contextualized three levels (security, political and economic) of engagement between AU and India under wider canvas of AU's interface with the extra-regional powers.

The research objectives of the project are fourfold: a) to understand AU's interrelationship with the African state system, b) to evaluate AU's approach towards existing and emerging faultlines in Africa, c) to assess AU's interrelationship with other regional groups across the African continent, and d) to explore the contours, constraints and capacities of the interface among the AU leadership, its member countries and the emerging extra-regional powers, including India.

The corollary research questions are: a) What is the nature of interrelationship between AU and the African state system? b) How is AU responding to African fault lines such as ethnic, religious, political, security, economic and strategic? c) How is AU negotiating with other regional groups across the African continent? d) What is the nature of interface between AU and India under wider context of extra-regional powers' interests in Africa?

The AU is perceived as a Pan-African entity with its mandate for 'comprehensive security' in the continent, implying its pursuit of three security objectives: resolution of armed conflicts, political stability and economic security. The investigative exercise of the project is based on 'content analysis' method. While the historical part of the analysis draws upon secondary sources (literature on Pan-Africanism and OAU), the contemporary part of the study uses both primary and secondary sources (official documents of and literature on AU). The case studies on territorial, political and economic security concerns are undertaken.

In pursuance of this study, a field work is undertaken for a interaction with concerned policy makers, analysts and academic experts based in AU headquarters, Organization for Social Science Research in Eastern and Southern Africa, Institute for Peace and Security Studies, Addis Ababa University and Wolkite University in Ethiopia.

The AU's interrelationship with the state system, existing and emerging social faultlines, and the multiple regional processes in Africa are interrogated. The findings of this analysis are used to explore the scope for policy improvisation pertaining to the interface among the AU, its member countries and the emerging extra-regional powers, including India.

Chapter – 1

Pan-African Security Architecture: AU's Role and Responsibility

The regional identity formation is underpinned by a process that involves a group of states and people identifying a set of common problems linked to their geographic space and finding solutions to these problems somewhere in between individual state initiative and the larger global intervention. The regional community's assertion of its own identity is, many a time, perceived as a response to the categorization it is historically subjected to by the extra-regional powers which are entrenched in the region. Regional resurgence in Africa is one such process of self-construction of identity and its institutional manifestation is reflected in the African Union's (AU) evolution based on the premise of 'African solution to the African problem.' A continent wide grouping of as many as 54 member states, the regional institution has completed fifty years of its existence, with formation of the Organisation of African Unity (OAU) in 1963 and its reformation into the AU in 2002, demonstrating phenomenal resilience and resurgence.

Keeping this in perspective, the chapter has reviewed the historicity of Pan-African movement that has led to the evolution of continental level security architecture. It has consequently assessed on the AU's role and responsibility as a comprehensive security provider in Africa.

Understanding a Region

Region is a complex concept with definitional multiplicity. Two significant features which lend meaning to a region are: (a) geographical proximity and (b) patterns of relations or interactions which posit a degree of regularity and intensity. While the first focuses on the physical dimensions of the region;

the second goes beyond geographical specifies. Bruce Russett uses five criteria for defining an international region: a) social and cultural homogeneity; b) shared political attitudes and behavior; c) shared institutional memberships; d) economic interdependence; and e) geographical proximity.[1] Thus, Russet defines a region based on such criteria as social mores, cultural heritage, political expectations, memberships, goods and services, and borders.[2] Louis Cantori and Steven Spiegel define an international region in terms of geography; social, economic, political, and organizational bonds; communications; levels of power; and structure of relations.[3] Comparing these two definitions, Jack Schick indicates that Cantori's and Spiegel's definition is more substantive, suggesting in addition to the criteria Russett uses that anti-colonialism or anti-imperialism may be what holds a region together.[4] Regional construction in Africa, having an intense anti-colonial engagement, can be understood in the wider notion of 'Southern Regionalism.'

The idea and process of regionalism in the South is underpinned by developmental quest through reinvigorating pursuit of regional connectivity on social, political, economic and strategic areas. The evolving congruence in these regions, based on geographic proximity and experiential linkages, have been intervened by arbitrary territorial demarcation through imposition of colonial statehood, asymmetrical production linkages with the capitalist North, Cold War encampments of the super powers and post-Cold War reinforcement of perceived indispensability of Atlantic norms and practices. The ideational and material triumphalism of the North has, however, encountered with the parallel trend towards a partial rise of the South, a drift that is primarily driven by Afro-Asian resurgence. The tectonic shift in the global strategic landscape under the current phase of globalization has indeed created a greater scope for consolidation of alternative endeavours of development in Africa and Asia, which can be best pursued at the regional levels.

Regionalism, Regionalization and Integration

What was initially labelled as "open" regionalism refers to the wave of regionalization that started gathering momentum in the late 1980s, as trade liberalization policies unleashed the expansion of cross border networks and transnational interactions powered by non-state players. As the term new regionalism gained currency, it acted mostly as a metaphor for discussing issues and addressing debates that were side-tracked when referring to regional economic, political, or military *integration*.[5] The revival of regionalism was a global and largely unanticipated phenomenon. The *de facto* crystallization of trade and investment flows around the three core regions of the triad (the Americas, Europe and North-East Asia) owed much to the dynamism of non-state players. When states were a driving force, this went along with significant policy-shifts in the mandates and agendas of established regional inter-governmental organizations.[6]

While the implementation of the EU's Single European Market agenda (1986–1992) went on, in North America, negotiations towards the North American Free Trade Area (NAFTA) (1991–1994) were proceeding. As this momentum gathered stamina, the establishment of the World Trade Organization (WTO) in 1994 stimulated fresh debates on regionalism as a master or servant of multilateralism.[7] Some scholars depicted regional trade arrangements, particularly those permitted under Article 24 of the GATT, as a stepping stone to further international liberalization,[8] while others viewed trading blocs as a threat to the multilateral trading order.[9]

In Latin America and in Asia, trade liberalization provided the impetus for rejuvenated agendas and the emergence of such new organizations as Mercosur.[1] This ongoing wave of regionalism, also branded as "new" regionalism, was frequently associated with an acknowledgement of less state- and euro-centric patterns of region-building. The contribution of such non state actors as the diasporas or private firms was reassessed and heavy reliance on institution-building and rule of law, as in Europe, was no longer considered as the only viable path towards integration. Unlike what was being observed elsewhere, Africa would, however, depart from this overall trend: the European experience and its commitment to the pooling of sovereignties remained the model of choice.

Another legacy from these years is the now well-established analytical distinction drawn between regionalism and regionalization. Regionalism refers to cognitive or institutionalized (state-centric) projects, while regionalization points to processes and to de facto outcomes. More specifically, regionalism can proceed from ideas or ideologies, programs, policies and goals that seek to transform an identified social space into a regional project. Since regionalism postulates the implementation of a program and the delineation of a strategy, it is often associated with institution-building or the conclusion of formal agreements. Regionalism can also relate to the production, invention or re-invention of transnational identities, a process concomitant with the delineation of mental maps and boundaries.

The notion of regionalism offers a long overdue insight into the paradox whereby, as Axline already lamented in the 1970s, "most cases of regional integration are among Third World countries, yet research in this field has been dominated by theory based on the European experience".[10] Regionalism accommodates an extreme heterogeneity of configurations, ranging from those involving the material organization of transfers of sovereignty (regional integration) to cognitive and ideational projects (associated with the invention of regions and construction of identities within existing states). Regionalism can account for integration processes, but can equally serve to monitor disintegration, namely demands that challenge state sovereignty and border-lines. Unlike the notion of regional integration, regionalism can account for agendas which, as the track-record of ASEAN illustrates, seek to promote region-building through sovereignty enhancement as opposed to sovereignty pooling.[11]

Regionalism also enables the analyst to keep away from an underlying assumption associated with the concept of regional economic integration, e.g. the confusion generated by its undifferentiated association with goals and processes.[12] By contrast, the dichotomy between regionalism and regionalization enables the analyst to account for configurations where, as is frequently the case in Africa, regionalism and regionalization contribute to shape distinct regional landscapes. Regionalization focuses on the build up of interactions which may or may not relate to an explicitly asserted or acknowledged formal regionalist project. Regionalization is a more encompassing notion than regionalism, since it takes into account processes and configurations where states are frequently not the key players. Regionalization may correlate with the regionalism's more formal arrangements or translate into processes of cross border economic integration. Regionalism may equally, as mentioned above, involve a loss of state territorial control and the emergence of autonomous regional spaces.

Thus, while regionalism is typically a top-down led phenomenon, closely associated with the evolution of regional integration in Europe, which started with the European Coal and Steel Community and progressed to the European Union, regionalization envelops formal and informal processes, but with an strong bottom-up component. Regionalization can grow irrespective of state policies, and even at time, in opposition to the purpose of the state.

In West Africa as in Asia, trade or migration networks do not have the ambition to build regional integration per se. It does, nonetheless promote regionalization. The Yoruba or Hausa trade diasporas in West Africa promote regionalization. The proceeds from the aggregation of the strategies of micro-economic agents promote regionalization.[13] Regionalization can also be the outcome of corporate strategies by firms, ranging from small business ventures to the large multinationals, seeking to enhance their competitive position. As Christopher Clapham observed:

> The model of inter-state integration through formal institutional framework which has hitherto dominated the analysis of integration in Africa and elsewhere has increasingly been challenged by the declining control of states over their own territories, the proliferation of informal networks, and the incorporation of Africa (on a highly subordinate basis) into the emerging global order.[14]

In West Africa, during that same decade, the spill-over effects of Charles Taylor's insurgency in Liberia would eventually destabilize the entire region. As analyzed by Hentz and Blevins in *Routledge Handbook of African Security*,[15] weak control over the borderlands of Liberia, Sierra Leone, Côte d'Ivoire or Guinea contributed to shape the contours of a conflict zone that was beyond the reach of any of them. In Central Africa too, the Great Lakes region offered an even more powerful example – the Rwanda genocide of 1994 may have been the immediate trigger, but the conflicts in the eastern DRC were only the latest round of a long-running regional conflict.

Also, in Africa the movement and displacement of people has been both a product of and a cause of regional conflict. Refugee populations promote their own brand of regionalization as they seek shelter across the border-line. Their inflow may also, as Karen Jacobsen argues, create national security problems by importing the conflict from their homelands (2001). The US State Failure Task Force stressed along this vein that external factors, including refugee movements can also increase the risk of state failure.[16]

Thirty-nine Sub-Saharan countries hosted more than one thousand refugees between 1990 and 1997. Almost all of these were compelled to migrate by some form of conflict, ranging from political or ethnic tensions to rebel insurgencies or conflict with neighboring states.[17] Twenty-eight countries hosted more than 20,000 refugees each. In Sudan, for instance, the Sudan People's Liberation Army (SPLA), then a rebel group, recruited internally displaced Sudanese from refugee camps to fight the government forces.[18] Likewise, Guinea's and Côte d'Ivoire's rebel forces drew their recruits from Liberian refugee camps. It is after neighboring countries Rwanda and Burundi had experienced brutal civil wars, that the DRC encountered a large influx of refugees. As militants that had committed genocide in Rwanda hid among them, this prompted the Rwandan government forces and rebel groups to intervene in Eastern DRC.[19]

As these instances illustrate, regionalization refers to the build up of interactions which do not necessary relate to an explicitly asserted or acknowledged regionalist project. Regionalization can build up irrespective of state policies, and even at times in opposition to their stated purpose. The disconnection between state-centred regionalism and de facto regionalization can reach exacerbated proportions in such a context. In Eastern Asia, China's emergence as a regional hub for trade and investment has kept building up despite a highly unfavorable politico-institutional environment. As also observed in Africa, trade or religious networks can also shape regional spaces based on social interactions that cut across political frontiers without necessarily challenging the preservation of the territorial *status quo*.[20]

Imperatives for OAU

The genesis of Africa's quest for an empowering identity can be traced to Pan-Africanist movements which initially began in late Nineteenth Century USA. Alienated in exploitative surroundings of the USA, the black races stood for equality among races and unity of the black races. Celebrated leaders of Pan-Africanism including Sylvester Williams, Marcus Garvey and W.E.B. Dubois worked tirelessly to promote the causes of the oppressed black races in the USA in the last century. In the post war years, Pan-Africanist visionaries like Kwame Nkrumah, independent Ghana's first Prime Minister and later the first President (1957-66), gave boost to Pan-Africanism by writing influential books like "Africa Must Unite"[21] or "Neo-colonialism the Last Stage of Imperialism"[22] and by holding the first conference of eight independent African states in Accra in April 1958. The various groupings among African states such as Casablanca group of radical states or moderate Brazzaville group comprising 12 former French colonies and later Monrovia group overcame their differences to form the OAU in 1963.

Despite this, the OAU members continued to be internally divided in the context of the politics of Cold War between the then superpowers. Also, the erstwhile colonial powers like France continued to influence policies of the former French colonies. Nevertheless, there was consensus in the OAU on opposing imperio-racist powers as also on the principles such as non-interference, equality and respect for sovereignty in inter-state relations in Africa. There was also an agreement within the OAU over the principle of inviolability of the then existing frontiers. The OAU, therefore, legitimised frontiers drawn by the colonial powers in the Berlin Conference of 1885 during the scramble for Africa. Evidently, the OAU's capacity to intervene in the domestic affairs of countries which witnessed civil wars (Chad 1981-82), genocide (Rwanda 1990-93) or gross violation of human rights (Uganda under Idi Amin 1971-1979) was severely circumscribed.[23]

The OAU had relentlessly championed the cause of anti-racist and anti-colonial struggles in Africa through its liberation committee and had even provided observer status to African National Congress (ANC) of South Africa within the OAU.

Before the formation of the OAU, George Padmore,[24] scholar-practitioner from Ghana with West Indian origin published his celebrated work, *Pan Africanism or Communism,* in 1956. In his Book, he tried to unravel the historical and cultural complexities, which constituted the 'racial dimension' of the Negritude movement and inhibited the black Africans from categorically associating themselves with international ideologies like Capitalism or Communism. He posed the dilemma of clashing options, i.e. Pan Africanism or Communism, before the emerging African states, and resolved in favour of the former.

After 25 years of the OAU's formation, an Indian Africanist Rajen Harshe in his Article *Reflections on the Organisation of African Unity* published in 1988 explained the OAU's vulnerability to powerful divisive forces, both endogenous and exogenous.[25] The endogenous forces have primarily stemmed from diverse foreign policy orientations of the member states, border disputes, ethnic and nationality problems. The involvements of exogenous forces such as the neo-colonial manoeuvring of erstwhile colonial powers and superpower rivalry have further divided the member states. Nevertheless, he also elucidated a commendable staying power that OAU has demonstrated amid the conflict-ridden situation that the continent was subjected to.

Imperatives for AU

With the end of the colonial rule and white minority/apartheid regimes in Zimbabwe (1980), Namibia (1990) and South Africa (1994), the AU is now primarily concerned about protecting dignity, integrity and independence of its member states while bolstering inter-state economic cooperation and promoting development through democratic, constitutional and peaceful means. The quest for democracy is demonstrated across Africa. There is a growing consensus among member countries towards AU's priority attention on political stability, which partly contributes to an economic growth of average 4.8 to 5.1 per cent that the continent has witnessed over the years. Endowed with precious sub-soil commodities and with huge reservoir of untapped land and other resources, Africa has evoked renewed interest of the external actors.[26]

The AU charter has equipped the member states better in terms of handling conflict related problems through collective action. Consequently, the AU states legitimately and frequently deploy pan-African force to intervene in the conflict theatres. The relatively powerful states like Nigeria contribute greater to the pan-African force. The collective action over issues like mushrooming of child soldiers, drug trafficking, illicit small arms trade and money laundering etc are also being gradually handled under the support of the AU more effectively. Furthermore, in the process of meeting the developmental challenges, the AU now is encouraging and incorporating the functioning of regional economic communities in various parts including Economic Community of West Africa (ECOWAS), primarily led by Nigeria, or Southern African Development Community (SADC), led by South Africa, more emphatically in its fold in an increasingly globalising world. Though regionally dominant states like South Africa or Nigeria draw greater advantages owing to their preponderant positions, regional groupings offer economies of scale and promote business synergy in their respective regions.

The AU plays a crucial role in developing Africa's partnerships with the rest of the world aimed at enhancing cooperation and consolidating growth of the continent. The African Union Partners Group (AUPG),[27] which is a platform of the concerned extra-regional economic partners of Africa, meets periodically in AU headquarters in Addis Ababa. The AU has, therefore, become a nodal point for the extra-regional economic powers, which attempt to engage Africa through continental approach. The Africa-Europe Partnership, the China-Africa Forum, the TICAD process led by

Japan, Africa-South America and Africa-Turkey partnerships and India-Africa Forum Summit (IAFS) are significant examples of this process.

India is a member of the AUPG. It held its first IAFS in New Delhi in April 2008. The Summit, attended by the countries representing AU and the Regional Economic Communities of Africa, adopted the Delhi Declaration and the Africa-India Framework for Cooperation, which constituted the blueprint for cooperation between India and Africa in the 21st century. The second IAFS was held in Addis Ababa in May 2011, as a continuation of commitment for partnership as espoused in the first IAFS. Each of the two Summits was followed by Joint Action Plans of both the Indian Government and the AU Commission. While India announced US$ 5.4 billion Lines of Credit (LoC) at the first IAFS Summit, it unveiled another package in the second Summit worth US$ 6 billion for Africa, including a US$ 5 billion LoC for the next three years, an additional US$ 700 million for establishing new institutions and organising training programmes and US$ 300 million to support the development of a new Ethiopia-Djibouti rail line.

Capacity building represents a major thrust area of the India-Africa development co-operation. India is setting up, under IAFS process, a host of institutions in African countries on bilateral, regional and Pan-African basis through a consultative approach, in which the AU's decision has been given the primacy. These institutions include four Pan-African institutes such as India-Africa Institute of Foreign Trade, Uganda, India-Africa Institute of Information Technology, Ghana, India-Africa Diamond Institute, Botswana and India-Africa Institute of Education, Planning and Administration, Burundi.

India stands for 'African Solution to the African Problem' principle and supports peaceful and consensual resolution of conflicts in Africa through the AU-led mediation process, even if it unfolds under the UN mandate. New Delhi wants pursuit of dialogue based conflict resolution method, by respecting sovereignty, integrity and unity of the African countries as well as being sensitive towards the legitimate aspirations of their people.

In the current context, Timothy Murithi in his Book *The African Union: Pan-Africanism, Peacebuilding and Development,* published in 2005 argued that the AU represents the third phase of the institutionalization of Pan-Africanism. He assessed the AU's peace and security institutions and analyzed as to how it is beginning to collaborate with civil society. He took a critical look at the AU's New Partnership for Africa's Development (NEPAD) and argued for its adoption of a developmental and governance agenda in Africa.[28]

Similarly, Samuel M. Makinda and F. Wafula Okumu in their work *The African Union: Challenges of Globalization, Security and Governance* published in 2007 showed as to how AU can effectively address the challenges of building and sustaining governance institutions and security mechanisms only if it has strategic leadership. Current debates on, and criticisms of, leadership in Africa are also analyzed as well as key options for overcoming the constraints that African leaders face.[29]

Olayiwola Abegunrin in his Book *Africa in Global Politics in the Twenty-First Century: A Pan-African Perspective* published in 2009 perceived Africa as a major player in the global affairs through the prisms of Nigeria and South Africa, which position themselves as two leading countries in the continent.[30] The sub-regional and continental organizations such as SADC and OAU/AU are analysed in this Book.

AU as a Norm Provider

Timothy Murithi has described AU as a norm entrepreneur in terms of its shift in agenda from Pan-Africanism to regional integration.[31] An endeavour to re-animate Pan-Africanism was the directing force behind the establishment of the African Union.[32] Pan-Africanism is an invented notion, but with the purpose of addressing Africa's insecurity and under development.[33] The ideal of African solidarity was first institutionalized in the form of the Organization of African Unity (OAU) in 1963, and subsequently re-articulated in the establishment of the AU in 2002. It continues to act as the animating drive behind the AU and its commitment to regional integration. However, the first ten years of the AU reveal that the Pan-Africanist project remains predominantly a top-down affair with elites from across Africa crafting and moulding the institutions to govern the continent, often without sufficiently consulting their publics. That said, there are social movements developing across African borders, which are also fuelling Pan-Africanism from below.[34]

In the ten years of its existence, the AU has attempted to play a continental role as a norm entrepreneur, understood here as a normative leader who encourages others to uphold a range of norms for the improvement of the livelihood of people within their jurisdiction or authority. The AU has sought to advance norms related to peace and stability and to function as a collective security regime. The AU Constitutive Act ascribes to the Union the right to intervene and a responsibility to protect in situations of war crimes, crimes against humanity, and genocide. In terms of norms and policy this means that African countries have to agree to pool their sovereignty to enable the AU to act as the continental guarantor and protector of the security, rights, and well-being of the African people.[35]

The African Union Peace and Security Council (PSC) was established as a legal institution of the Union through the 'Protocol Relating to the Establishment of the Peace and Security Council of the African Union' I 2002, and in this sense the AU has undoubtedly led in promoting the norms of peace and security on the continent. Currently the AU is seeking to operationalize these norms through its peace operations in Somalia, the African Union Mission in Somalia (AMISOM, launched in 2007), its Electoral and Security Assistance Mission to the Comoros (AU-MAES, launched in 2008), and its contribution to the Joint AU-UN Hybrid Mission in Darfur (UNAMID, launched in 2007). In addition, Union personnel contributed towards stabilizing the situation in Burundi, through the AU Mission in Burundi (AMIB) from 2003 to 2004.[36]

Agenda 2063

Agenda 2063 is a strategic framework for the socio-economic transformation of the continent over the next 50 years. It builds on, and seeks to accelerate the implementation of the past and existing continental initiatives developed at national, regional and continental levels to ensure growth and sustainable development. It is a continuation of the pan-African drive over centuries, for unity, self-determination, freedom, progress and collective prosperity pursued under Pan-Africanism and African Renaissance. It was agreed upon by the African leaders in 2013 during the 50th Anniversary of the Organization of African Unity (OAU). Therefore, it should be understood in that context.[37]

The term Pan-Africanism was first used by Henry Sylvester William who organized the first pan-African congress in 1900 in the United Kingdom. On the conviction that all Africans had a common destiny, it later on developed as a world-wide Pan-African Movement that aimed at bringing together and unite all Africans wherever they were to emancipate themselves from sufferings of slavery, colonialism, economic exploitation, racial discrimination etc. In the process, there also developed the term African Renaissance conceptualized by Cheikh Anta Diop in 1946 who contended that Africans could overcome the challenges they were experiencing and would be able to transform themselves by re-birth of their cultures, societies, values and socio-economic progress.

Thus, Pan-Africanism and African Renaissance progressed as an ambition ideology of Africans whose first concrete result was the creation of the OAU in 1963 to realize its objectives. It has continued to be promoted by many people and institutions in various ways, including the African Union that designated 2013 as the year of Pan-Africanism and African Renaissance. The decision was reached because 2013 coincided with the 50th Anniversary of the OAU; and the African leaders wanted to seize the opportunity to reflect on the past, re-kindle its ideals and plan for the better future of Africa and its people.

The move was informed by the fact that when the OAU was established in 1963, there were many challenges that had first to be overcome. Firstly, almost half of the continent was still under colonialism; other African countries that were free were still internally not well organized; relations with the regional groupings (today Regional Economic Communities—RECs) had not been laid down and strengthened, and people's involvement not yet properly strategized. As a result, there was no common vision, hence no clear strategy, on how to pursue the OAU objectives, among which fundamentally was the African unity agenda and generally on how to advance Pan-Africanism and African Renaissance.[38]

In the circumstances, member states had first to focus on the liberation of the continent, strengthening RECs and nation-building, and so on. This affected most of the socio-economic strategies laid down at that time, as they were of short-term and not very well conceived. For instance, they did not involve fundamental stakeholders—African citizenry and their grassroots institutions—other important elements such as reliable sources of funding, constant monitoring and evaluation strategies etc. The situation led to many plans and decisions taken under the OAU to be ineffectively executed with limited or no anticipated results at all.

By 2013, the African Union (AU) found itself in a new conducive environment for taking bold steps to advance the socio-economic development and integration of the continent through a long-term planning. For instance, colonialism had been greatly defeated and apartheid dismantled. Member states were better organized with major advances in many areas such as in conflict management and resolution, and good governance where the important role of civil society and ordinary people started to be recognized. In addition, consensus had been reached on making the better-organized RECs pillars of the continental organization; and most important, member states had agreed on a common vision of "an integrated, prosperous and peaceful Africa, driven and managed by its own citizens and representing a dynamic force in the international arena." Meanwhile, good experience had also been gained in running successfully continent-wide blueprints, like the New Partnership for Africa's Development (NEPAD).

Furthermore, there have emerged other new factors to Africa's advantage. They included development and investment opportunities that have started seeing many African countries economically booming; emergence of new international alliances, like that of Brazil, Russia, India, China and South Africa (BRICS); and in general the changing of universal context of globalization and revolution in information technology, and so on. Therefore, by 2013, it was high time that the Africa Union developed a long-term strategy that would harmonize and integrate all plans and frameworks available at national, regional and continental levels under one umbrella for their successful execution in order to advance integration in Africa.[39]

Consequently, during the OAU Golden Jubilee, the African leaders adopted the 50th Anniversary Solemn Declaration in which they identified eight priority areas to focus their attention. They pledged to integrate them in their national plans and in the development of the Continental Agenda 2063 through a people-driven process. The eight areas were: i) African Identity and Renaissance, ii) to continue the struggle against colonialism and the right to self-determination of people still under colonial rule, iii) the Integration Agenda, iv) social and economic development, v) Peace and Security Agenda, vi) Democratic Governance, vii) Determining Africa's Destiny, viii) Africa's Place in the World.

For the purpose of this meeting, and as far as peace and human security is concerned, the African leaders confirmed, in the Declaration, their determination to achieve the goal of a conflict-free Africa, to make peace a reality and to rid the continent of wars, civil conflicts, human rights violations, humanitarian disasters and violent conflicts, including prevention of genocide. They pledged "not to bequeath the burden of conflicts to the next generation of Africans and undertake to end all wars in Africa by 2020".

On the African Unity and Renaissance, the African Heads of State and Government committed themselves to accelerate the African Renaissance by ensuring the integration of the principles of Pan-Africanism in all policies and initiatives; and the promotion of people-to-people engagements, including youth and civil society exchanges in order to strengthen pan-Africanism. Thus, when one finds out that the principles of the African Solidarity Caravan which are to "reflect, connect, strategize, organize, mobilize, transform, consolidate and celebrate" sees this occasion to be at its proper place and timely to assist in advancing the Agenda 2063.[40]

In overall, Agenda 2063 was therefore intended to be a well-conceived plan for the realization of the common vision coming the next fifty years, when the AU will be celebrating the OAU Centenary. The choice of a fifty-year lifespan for the Agenda was also to offer an opportunity and enough time to build coherence for all the plans at all three levels (from national to continental) and bring them under one framework. This is because presently member states have plans with different lifespans (some 40 years, others targeting 2050, while others less). Furthermore, such a long-term strategy is an experience that has been successfully tried in countries like China.

The task of developing the Agenda 2063 was entrusted to the African Union Commission, working with NEPAD Coordinating Agency (NPCA) and in close collaboration with the African Development Bank (AFDB) and the United Nations Economic Commission for Africa (UNECA). It is being undertaken and coordinated in the Office of the Chairperson of the AU Commission, under the Directorate of the Strategic Policy Planning, Monitoring, Evaluation and Resource Mobilization (SPPMERM).

The technical process has been covering analytical work and consultations in almost all sectors. Specifically, the analytical work has involved the review of national plans (about 38 member states), regional (RECs) and continental frameworks such as Programme for Infrastructure and Development in Africa (PIDA), Comprehensive African Agricultural Development Plan (CAADP), Accelerated Industrial Development in Africa (AIDA), the Abuja Treaty etc. [41]

With regard to consultations for the collection of opinion from the African people, extensive meetings with key stakeholders, namely, African people of nearly all categories—youth, women, civil society, including those in the Diaspora and just recently faith-based groups—RECs and AU organs have been undertaken. From them, seven aspirations were distilled that the African citizenry wanted to see pursued in the Agenda 2063. They were: i) a prosperous Africa based on inclusive growth and sustainable development, ii) an integrated continent, politically united, and based on the ideals of Pan Africanism, iii) an Africa of good governance, respect for human rights, justice and the rule of law, iv) a peaceful and secure Africa - free of conflict and at peace with itself, v) an Africa with a strong cultural identity, values and ethics, vi) an Africa whose development is people-driven, especially relying on the potential offered by its youth and women, vii) Africa as a strong and influential global player and partner. The seven aspirations have, therefore, formed the fundamental basis on which the Agenda 2063 framework document and all its various components, like the Agenda 2063 Popular Version: Africa We Want; Communication Strategy; First Ten-Year Implementation Plan; Monitoring and Evaluation Strategy as well Resource Mobilization Strategy etc., have been developed and most of them submitted to the policy organs.

The documents have elaborated for each aspiration its goals, targets, priority areas and strategies for their realization to be achieved in phases starting with the first ten years and beyond to 2063. The AU has developed targets under Aspiration Four regarding peace and security to be: self-reliance in funding Africa's Peace and security institutions; well equipped, competent regional and continental security structures/mechanisms to deal with emerging security threats; capable, equipped and professional security forces with continental capabilities; self-sufficient defence industry. Under Aspiration Six, concerning an Africa whose development is people-driven by relying on the full potential offered by its youth and women, it has developed two goals, namely, full gender equality in all spheres of life; and engaged and empowered youth and children, and so on.

In view of the foregoing, Agenda 2063, besides the Constitutive Act of the African Union being the basic legal instrument of the Union, it is basically built on the AU Vision; the 50th Anniversary Solemn Declaration, the seven aspirations of African people and frameworks already adopted. The critical success factors for Agenda 2063 are:

i)   Transformational leadership: need for transformational leadership in all fields and at all levels,

ii) Political commitment to implementing the plan,

iii) African unity and solidarity.

Agenda 2063 reaffirming African unity and solidarity in the face of continued external interference including by multi-national corporations attempts to divide the continent and undue pressures and illegal sanctions on some countries, iv) participation and inclusion of all stakeholders in the conception, design, implementation, monitoring and evaluation as a critical success factor, enhancing awareness and ownership and knowledge of Agenda 2063, thereby solidify collective commitments to implementing it. Agenda 2063 very much depends, therefore, on its envisaged main actors which are AU and its Organs, RECs, member states, African citizenry at large represented in various forms, including the African civil society, and the Diaspora etc. These are in addition to close collaborators, the AfDB and UNECA, and other partners.[42]

Ideational Underpinning for African Integration

Ideas and processes remain inextricably linked in Africa's tryst with its political development. Nurturing strong quest for 'democratic entitlements,' African people pursue their course of political development amid the historical encounter with a series of disruptive realities. These include imposition of colonial statehood through arbitrary territorial demarcation, Cold War encampments of the super powers containing functional interface between the governing elites   and the citizenry thereby restricting societal cohesion, externally imposed multi-party system, competition between traditional (Western) and emerging extra-regional powers for economic space, use of political dissent as strategic opportunity by the Western actors, selective unilateral interventions or threat of such interventions by these actors in the guise of 'humanitarian' mandate, partisan dereliction of the domestic political dispensation and ethno-electoral violent contestation. The cumulative complexity of the politico-security milieu is, however, paralleled by self-corrective trends such as inclination for institutionalized domestic power transition, panel of the wise practice and, above all, effective regional mediation in Africa.

The popular aspiration of a 'substantively free and self-sustained' Africa can, indeed, be discerned in the profound ideas of many thinkers who carry meaningful locational connectivity with the continent and also have intense functional interface with the world external to it. The path-breaking propositions of *Pan-Africanism or Communism* by George Padmore, *African Liberalism* by Ali Mazrui and *Sovereignty as Responsibility* by Francis

Deng are salient representative of such genre of thought reflecting constant developmental endeavours of African people in the decisive stages of their political struggle.

First, George Padmore's celebrated work titled *Pan-Africanism or Communism? The Coming Struggle for Africa*, with foreword by Richard Wright, was published by D. Dobson in London in 1956. The substance of Padmore's argument is that Western Communist Parties made their attitude to the struggles of the African people subordinate to the foreign policy interests of the Soviet Union; and that the Soviet Union made cynical use of the African people's struggles for its own ends. He was concerned to mark out a path for Africa's future- and that path, in Padmore's view, should above all avoid any alliance with the Soviet Union or with individual Communist Parties. He combines his anti-Communism and anti-Sovietism with the argument that the European working class has become corrupt and its 'revolutionary ardor' has been blunted. Padmore tries to bring Lenin to his aid in support of this argument, citing his comments about a 'bourgeoisified' working class.[43] Prof. Nwafor rightly commented that Padmore's ideas of "Pan-Africanism were admirably suited to the era of the cold war during which most African countries emerged into independence."[45]

Padmore's work remains a remarkable tract for the times, with revealing resentment of the way Stalinists had violated the right of Africans to 'mental freedom.'[46] He wrote, "The only force capable of containing Communism in Asia and Africa is dynamic nationalism based upon a socialist programme of industrialization and co-operative methods of agricultural production."[47] Communists, according to Padmore, are 'more interested in promoting the foreign policies of the Soviet Union than in advancing the national liberation of...dependent countries.'[48] The 'greatest psychological mistake' made by the West, however, is in failing to realize that African leaders are determined 'to be mentally free from the dictation of Europeans, regardless of their ideology',[49] an attitude dramatically underlined at Bandung and subsequently.[50]

Ali Mazrui propounded the idea of *African Liberalism* in his article titled *Africa, My Conscience and I.* Writing it in *Transition* journal in the year 1974, he conceived *African Liberalism* as "a toleration of diversity and pluralism in the society, a re-duction of governmental arbitrariness, a respect for intellectual non-conformity, some degree of responsiveness to public opinion, some degree of accountability to the electorate, and a relatively fair chance for those who are out of government to campaign to discredit the government and hopefully prepare the way for their own triumph."

Mazrui gave the reason for the probable discredit of 'Liberalism in Africa' by saying, "it came with capitalism, and capitalism for Africans was discredited mainly because it came with imperialism." He argued that "it is possible to have capitalism without liberalism, as examples in places like Brazil, Spain and Portugal before the coup would indicate. But is it possible to have liberalism without capitalism?" "Scandinavian countries are amongst the most liberal in the world in the freedoms they give to individuals ranging from free speech to free love," according to him, "and yet the Scandinavian countries have also achieved some substantial controls over their capitalism." He added, "Capitalism to some extent has been tamed, socialized, and more deeply liberalized in those conditions."[51]

Mazrui identified four types of capitalism - ascriptive, liberal, fascist and state capitalism. Ascriptive capitalism tends to give special concessions to heredity and birth, extending entrepreneurial opportunities to younger sons of the aristocracy, be that aristocracy based on ethnicity, caste or other forms of descent. England in much of the eighteenth century illustrated the phenomenon of ascriptive capitalism, reserving major opportunities of investment and economic success to those who were well born. By the second half of the nineteenth century, England was getting liberalised, and opening up the doors of economic success to strata of society which had previously been relegated to less triumphant levels. While retaining some ascriptive elements in the British economic and political system, the liberalism has widened the power of trade unions, reduced the control of the House of Lords and aristocracy, diluted the power of the monarchy, expanded the powers of the middle classes, and facilitated the processes of social mobility, both upwards and downwards. Japanese capitalism remained substantially ascriptive well into the twentieth century. Ascriptive capitalism fuses itself with some elements of feudalism. Capitalism based on a caste system is also ascriptive.[52]

Kenya's capitalism is partly liberal and partly ascriptive, according to Mazrui. Its western orientation gave it a liberal bias. Its leadership by the Kikuyu gave it an ascriptive tendency. The United States was born on a doctrine of liberal capitalism, with a profound distrust of a landed aristocracy and a commitment to the principle of social mobility. Again the United States' performance for the first a hundred and fifty years of its life far from fulfilled the ultimate goals of its own political culture. But there is no doubt that while British capitalism started with a massive bias on the side of ascription, American capitalism was born with a bias towards liberalism.[53]

Capitalism as a fascist phenomenon belongs to the twentieth century, with the notion of an authoritarian or totalitarian polity based on corporate economic interests in a special alliance of production. It is clear that Hitler's Germany, Mussolini's Italy, and Salazar's Portugal, while basically capitalistic, were normatively different from Churchill's England or Roosevelt's America. The latter two included a greater distrust of governmental arbitrariness, some respect for individual and civil liberties, parliamentary or electoral accountability, and a highly articulate arena of public dissent. The Watergate scandal could never have been exposed in a fascist country without a revolution. The Watergate scandal has disgraced the United States; yet the very fact that it has been revealed so openly and mercilessly has been a credit to the American system of government. It is these considerations which make liberal capitalism under Richard Nixon qualitatively different from fascist capitalism under Adolf Hitler. Nixon himself as a personality may have a good deal in common with Hitler, but the American system of government has less in common with Nazi Germany.[54]

Finally, there is state capitalism, usually associated with countries claiming to be socialistic, and even Marxist. The state entered the scene to exploit the working man, partly in pursuit of the profit motive, and partly for the greater glory of the state. State capitalism produces a powerful bureaucratic class, often at least as ruthless and exploitative as any bourgeois class under the other forms of capitalism.[55]

Mazrui maintained that 'Liberalism in Africa' need not follow the western book of rules. There is a distinction, according to him, between liberal institutions and liberal rules. The institutions of western liberalism include in some cases a sovereign parliament, as in the United Kingdom, and in others, separation of powers between the legislature, the executive and judiciary, as in the United States. Sovereignty of parliament and separation of powers are mutually exclusive as institutional principles.[56]

The liberal rules of the game, on the other hand, are substantially similar in both the United Kingdom and the United States. They include precisely those principles of public accountability, toleration of dissent, respect for diversity and pluralism, and a profound abhorrence of unrestrained governmental arbitrariness. He believed that the liberal institutions as they have evolved in the western world are probably unsuitable for African conditions, and would have to be modified through a process of trial and error. African people might have to evolve different types of party systems, different rules of legislative behaviour, different boundaries of executive initiative, and different processes for the judiciary. But some residual control of authority, some residual public accountability-these are all indispensible liberal values, whether the arena is 'Africa, India, Western Europe, or North America.'[57]

In the years after independence many African intellectuals developed a new interest not only in socialism but also in Marxian vocabulary and symbolism as they sought to assert their intellectual and economic independence. It is true that the Marxian rhetoric and strategy could succeed in creating a mood of militant economic independence. But the use of Marxian ideas as a method of asserting African intellectual independence is basically a contradiction.[58]

On the other hand, many Africans resent the great cultural dominance that European civilisation has exerted over their lives. The range of this dominance is wide: European languages, educational systems, Gregorian calendar, time division, science and technology, dressing style. The alien influence in Africa is omnipresent. The massive presence of alien civilisations in the lives of Africans, especially the omnipresence of European civilisation, evokes their rebellion against this dependency and assertion for a militant autonomy. Since the different ideologies were quite capable of being abused by their adherents and perpetrators, Africa should seek to discover at least some truths on its own initiative instead of simply borrowing the rhetoric of European dissenters. It is necessary, according to Mazrui, for the African continent to have both a socialist Tanzania and a capitalist Kenya, and for its people to derive their own lessons from the two experiments in the full maturity of historical time.[59]

African liberal identity is partly subscribed to the African nationalist character. To the extent that liberalism at its most tolerant allows for diversity and experimentation, it is to liberalism that needs to be embraced, creating scope to experience the full impact of 'indigenous intellectual innovation'. By refusing to be a monopolistic system or a closed system, a liberal Africa would permit itself to be stimulated even by the enemies of liberalism. It could respond to a variety of intellectual traditions, from Islam to Marxism, from

Judeo-Christian concepts to the domestic heritage of the African continent itself.[60]

In liberal societies which sincerely uphold their values, Marxist books and ideas compete in the open market. Marxist newspapers are freely published, communist parties are formed, and individual communists can attain national pre-eminence. By contrast, communist systems rarely allow similar latitude to those of their nationals who might prefer the values of liberalism or capitalism, or indeed of some alternative Marxist tradition divergent from the official one in their own country. Feeling the heavy burden of external intellectual dominance, African continent has to permit itself the possibility of indigenous experimentation in diversity, rather than enslave itself to yet another 'foreign closed intellectual system'.[61]

But the liberalism which could serve Africa well must be only that part of the tradition which is concerned with the rules of the game, with permitting diversity and freedom of thought. The actual institutions of the liberal West need not be re-enacted in the African continent. Africa could hope for alternative institutions, but might nevertheless permit its scientists, philosophers, artists and traditional sages to contribute to a new cultural melting pot of their own. Liberalism in Africa has to be tamed and conditioned by African nationalism and third world solidarity.[62]

Mazrui's vision of an interface among African liberalism, African nationalism and third world solidarity is more widely elaborated in his article *Creative Eclectism as an Ideological Alternative: an African Perspective.* Writing it in *Alternative* journal in the year 1975, he stated that at least since the beginning of 20th century Africa has been an intellectual melting pot. In this essay, he mentioned that penetration of external intellectual influences, started earlier, gathered momentum more recently, and assumed most diverse forms in the last seventy to eighty years. Both Islam and Christianity as systems of ideas came to Africa from their earliest days. Ethiopia has been Christian longer than many parts of Europe, including England. And North Africa was substantially Islamized in the first century of Muhammad's religion, which later spread to other parts of the continent. Each had ideas and values which have direct political implications.[63]

After examining the role of culture in imperialism, the entry of liberal and capitalist values in Africa, the rise of modern nationalism, the fascination of Marxism among black intellectuals, and the obstinate resilience of many traditional African values, Mazrui came to the conclusion that creative eclecticism (implying a genius for selectivity, for synthesizing disparate elements, and for ultimate independent growth in the intellectual field) is the only ideological alternative compatible with African autonomy in modern conditions.[64] Envisioning his *African Liberal* worldview, Mazrui stated:

> I do have a vision of an African tomorrow that I have tried to transmit in both my teaching and my writings. It is a tomorrow which would permit Africa the full potential of intellectual diversity-which would tame our governments into accepting dissent, train outsiders into respecting our perspectives, educate our intellectuals into the habits of mental self-reliance, persuade our people to explore new horizons, and prepare ourselves for a new phase of indigenous creativity. That is my creed in all its painful naivet.[65]

In the 1990s, Francis Deng introduced the concept of 'sovereignty as responsibility' when working as special representative of the United Nations Secretary General on internally displaced persons. For Deng, sovereignty as responsibility meant that national governments were accountable to their own people and also to the international community for the provision of minimum standards of security and welfare for their citizens. In 2001, the International Commission on Intervention and State Sovereignty adopted Deng's concept and reframed it as 'the responsibility to protect/'. Sovereign states were said to be responsible to the international community for the protection of their populations from grave violations of human rights, and the international community, in turn, was bound to ensure that populations were protected.[66]

Francis Deng et al assert that sovereignty can no longer be seen as a protection against interference, but as a charge of responsibility where the state is accountable to both domestic and external constituencies. In internal conflicts in Africa, sovereign states have often failed to take responsibility for their own citizens' welfare and for the humanitarian consequences of conflict, leaving the victims with no assistance. It is shown how that responsibility can be exercised by states over their own population, and by other states in assistance to their fellow sovereigns. Sovereignty as Responsibility presents a framework that should guide both national governments and the international community in discharging their respective responsibilities. Broad principles are developed by examining identity as a potential source of conflict, governance as a matter of managing conflict, and economics as a policy field for deterring conflict.[67]

Considering conflict management, political stability, economic development, and social welfare as functions of governance, Francis Deng and his co-authors develop strategies, guidelines, and roles for its responsible exercise. Some African governments, such as South Africa in the 1990s and Ghana since 1980, have demonstrated impressive gains against these standards. Opportunities for making sovereignty more responsible and improving the management of conflicts are examined at the regional and international levels. The lessons from the mixed successes of regional conflict management actions, such as the West African intervention in Liberia, the East African mediation in Sudan, and international efforts to urge talks to end the conflict in Angola, indicate friends and neighbors outside the state in conflict have important roles to play in increasing sovereign responsibility.[68]

Approaching conflict management from the perspective of the 'responsibilities of sovereignty' provides a framework for evaluating government accountability. Standards are proposed for guiding performance and sharpening tools of conflict prevention rather than simply making post-hoc judgments on success or failure. Sovereign responsibility is demonstrated both as a national obligation and a global imperative.[69] Deng has mentioned criticality of a 'regional approach', by arguing that countries in the same region quite often share the problem. Crisis in one country overspills into the neighbouring countries in the form of refugees, carrying their baggage of political crisis, according to him, which can destabilise the whole region.[70]

Francis Deng has tried to bridge the gap between ideal aspirations and engagement with ground realities. To this end, he said that it is one thing to say to governments that in the name of human rights we will override their sovereignty; to threaten that if they violate human rights the world will move in and will stop them from doing it by whatever means necessary. It is another thing to say: 'Sovereignty itself means responsibility, and the dignity you enjoy in the international community, the respect you have, your legitimacy at home and abroad, has a lot to do with the degree to which you discharge the positive responsibilities of sovereignty.'[71]

The notion of sovereignty as responsibility has evolved into the responsibility to protect, with the three pillars: a) the responsibility of the state to protect its own populations, b) the responsibility of the international community to assist the state to enhance its capacity to discharge its national responsibility and c) the responsibility of the international community to take collective action under the UN Charter when a state is manifestly failing to protect its own populations. Measures under the third pillar range from diplomatic intercession to the imposition of sanctions, and, in extreme cases, to military intervention. The responsibility to protect is, however, being more and more seen, according to Deng, in terms of the third pillar, which is an absolute last resort of using coercive means to control the situation, even having under its ambit non-coercive measures to apply.[72]

Deng perceives gist of the African crisis being grounded in the mismanagement of diversity and not making use of the indigenous values and institutions as building blocks in the process of nation-building. The indigenous system of autonomy or political structures and processes was replaced by a centralized authority of the colonial state that raised the stakes in that the central authority became the key to acquiring power, services and opportunities for development. At independence, the central authority was captured by certain ethnic groups which then monopolized power and marginalized others. This struggle for central power became the key to the ongoing tensions and conflicts resulting in coups and counter coups and causing instability.[73]

There is a need for recognizing the realities of ethnic compositions, which have sustained the Africans for centuries, according to Deng, if not thousands of years. While ethnicity has been abused and manipulated by both the colonial authorities and independent governments, it is a potential resource for a genuinely de-centralized system of governance and development as a process of self-enhancement from within. In other words, ethnicity can be used as a means for divisiveness but it can also be used constructively as a means for grounding the system of governance and development in the African reality.[74]

Research Outlay

A careful scrutiny of the existing literature on the AU indicates that any holistic academic exercise of the subject is a rarity. The research project has tried to fill this analytical gap, by looking at the issue of Pan-African Regionalism from a comprehensive security perspective. It has also contextualized three levels (*security, political and economic*) of engagement between AU and India under wider canvas of AU's interface with the extra-regional powers. The research objectives of the project are fourfold: a) to understand AU's interrelationship with the African state system, b) to evaluate AU's approach towards existing and emerging faultlines in Africa, c) to assess AU's interrelationship with other regional groups across the African continent, and d) to explore the contours, constraints and capacities of the interface among the AU leadership, its member countries and the emerging extra-regional powers, including India. The corollary research questions are: a) What is the nature of interrelationship between AU and the African state system? b) How is AU responding to African fault lines such as ethnic, religious, political, security, economic and strategic? c) How is AU negotiating with other regional groups across the African continent? d) What is the nature of interface between AU and India under wider context of extra-regional powers' interests in Africa?

The AU is perceived as a Pan-African entity with its mandate for 'comprehensive security' in the continent, implying its pursuit of three security objectives: resolution of armed conflicts, political stability and economic security. The investigative exercise of the project is based on 'content analysis' method. While the historical part of the analysis draws upon secondary sources (literature on Pan-Africanism and OAU), the contemporary part of the study uses both primary and secondary sources (official documents of and literature on AU). The case studies on territorial, political and economic security concerns are undertaken. The AU's interrelationship with the state system, existing and emerging social faultlines, and the multiple regional processes in Africa are interrogated. The findings of this analysis are used to explore the scope for policy improvisation pertaining to the interface among the AU, its member countries and the emerging extra-regional powers, including India.

Endnotes

1   Bruce Russett (1967), *International Regions and the International System: A Study in Political Ecology* (Chicago; Rand McNally), chapters 1, 11, 12, 13.

2   Bruce Russett, "Delineating International Regions," Quantitative International Politics: Insights and Evidence (ed. J. David Singer) (New York: The Free Press, 1968), pp. 317-352.

3   Louis Cantori and Steven L. Spiegel, "International Regions: A Comparative Approach to Five Subordinate Systems," *International Studies Quarterly 13* (December, 1969), p. 362.

4   Jack M. Schick, "Conflict and Integration in the Near East: Regionalism and the Study of Crises," *Professional Paper No. 44, October 1970*, https://www.cna.org/sites/default/files/research/5500004400.pdf

5   Daniel C. Bach (2013), "Regionalism in Africa: Concepts and Context", in James J. Hentz (Ed.) *Routledge Handbook of African Security*, London: Routledge

6   Fawcett, Louise (1995) "Regionalism in historical perspective" in Fawcett, Louise and Andrew Hurrell, eds., (1995) Regionalism in World Politics: Regional organization and international order. Oxford: Oxford University Press, pp. 9-36.

7   Hveem, Helge (1999) "Political Regionalism: Master or Servant of Economic Internationalization?" in: Björn, Hettne; Andras, Inotai & Osvaldo, Sunkel, eds., Globalism and the New Regionalism, London: Macmillan, pp. 85-115.

8   Lawrence, R.Z. (1995), *Towards Free Trade in the Middle East: The Triad and Beyond*, Cambridge, Mass.: ISEPME, Harvard University; J. Vernon Henderson (1994), "Externalities and Industrial Development," *NBER Working Papers 4730*, National Bureau of Economic Research, Inc.

9   Thurow, Lester (1992), *Head to Head: The Coming Economic Battle Among Japan, Europe, and America*,   New York: William Morrow; Bhagwati, J. and Krueger, A. 1995, *The Dangerous Drift to Preferential Trade Agreements*, Washington DC: AEI Press.

10   Axline, Andrew W. (1977) "Underdevelopment, Dependence and Integration: The Politics of Regionalism in the Third world", *International Organization*, vol. XXXI, no. 1, p. 83.

11   Higgot, Richard (1995) "Economic co-operation in the Asia Pacific: A Theoretical Comparison with the European Union", Journal of European Public Policy, vol. 2, no. 3, pp. 361-363

12   Warleigh-Lack, Alex; Nick, Robinson & Ben, Rosamund , eds. (2010), New Regionalism and the European Union, Oxford, Routledge.

13   Soderbaum, F. and Taylor, I. 2008, *Afro-Regions: The Dynamics of Cross-Border Micro-Regionalism in Africa*, Uppsala: Nordic Africa Institute.

14   Christopher Clapham (1999), *African Guerrillas,* Bloomington: Indiana University Press, p.53.

15   Hentz and Blevins (2013), "States, Boundaries, and Regional Collapse in Sub-Saharan Africa" in James J. Hentz (Ed.) *Routledge Handbook of African Security,* London: Routledge

16   State Failure Task Force 2000

17   Jacobsen, K. (2001), "The Forgotten Solution: Local Integration for Refugees in Developing Countries," *New Issues in Refugee Research*, Working Paper No. 45, UNHCR

18   USCR 1997

19   Daniel C. Bach (2013), op.cit.

20   Ibid.

21   Kwame Nkrumah (1970), *Africa Must Unite*, New York: International Publishers, p.1.

22   Kwame Nkrumah (1965), *Neo-Colonialism: The Last Stage of Imperialism*, London: Thomas Nelson & Sons, Ltd., p.3.

23   Rajen Harshe (2013), "The African Union: A Critical Overview", http://www.irgamag.com/regions/africa/item/4211-*the-african-union-a-critical-overview

24   George Padmore (1956), Pan *Africanism or Communism?*: The Coming Struggle for Africa, London: D. Dobson.

25   Rajen Harshe, Reflections *on the Organisation of African Unity, Economic and Political Weekly*, 23 (8), 1988.

26   Ibid.

27 Government of India, MEA, India - African Union Relations, http://www.mea. gov.in/Portal/ForeignRelation/india-african-union-relations-march-2012.pdf,

28 Timothy Murithi (2005), *The African Union: Pan-Africanism, Peacebuilding and Development*, Aldershot: Ashgate, p.1.

29 Samuel M. Makinda and F. Wafula Okumu (2007), *The African Union: Challenges of Globalization, Security and Governance*, Oxon: Routledge, p. iv.

30 Olayiwola Abegunrin (2009), *Global Politics in the Twenty-First Century: A Pan-African Perspective*, New York: Palgrave Macmillan, p.vi.

31 Timothy Murithi, "Briefing the African Union at Ten: An Appraisal," *African Affairs*, 111(445), 2012, p.667.

32 Hakim Adi and Marika Sherwood (2003), *Pan-African History: Political figures from Africa and the Disapora since 1787*, London: Routledge, p. vii.

33 Timothy Murithi, 2005, op.cit.

34 Timothy Murithi, 2012, op.cit.

35 Ibid.

36 Ibid.

37 Kassim M. Khamis, "The African Union and the Renaissance of Africa: Assessing the Role of Civil Society and African People in Deepening and Supporting the AU's Agenda 2063", Presentation to the Peace and Human Security Festival, 04 December 2014, Addis Ababa, Ethiopia.

38 Ibid.

39 Ibid.

40 Ibid.

41 Ibid.

42 Ibid.

43 George Padmore (1956), *Pan-Africanism or Communism? The Coming Struggle for Africa*, London: D. Dobson, pp. 279-80.

44 Jack Woddis, "Pan-Africanism or Communism by George Padmore", *Science & Society*, 38 (1), Spring 1974, pp. 107-109.

45 John D. Hargreaves, "Padmore Classic: Pan-Africanism or Communism by George Padmore", *African Studies Review*, 15 (3), December 1972, pp. 519-520.

46 George Padmore (1956), op.cit., p. 339.

47 Ibid, p. 371.

48 Ibid, p. 342.

49 Kenneth Robinson, "Pan-Africanism or Communism? The Coming Struggle for Africa by George Padmore", *International Affairs*, 33 (2), April 1957, pp. 248-249.

50 Ali A. Mazrui, "Africa, My Conscience and I", *Transition*, 46, 1974, p. 68.

51 Ibid.

52 Ibid.

53 Ibid.

54 Ibid.

55 Ibid, p. 69.

56 Ibid.

57 Ibid.

58 Ibid.

59 Ibid.

60 Ibid.

61 Ibid,70.

62 Ali A. Mazrui, "Creative Eclectism as an Ideological Alternative: an African Perspective", *Alternative: Global, Local, Political*, 1 (4), December 1975, p. 465.

63 Ibid.

64 Op.cit., Mazrui (1974), p.71.

65 Luke Glanville, "Power and Responsibility: Building International Order in an Era of Transnational Threats by Bruce Jones; Carlos Pascual; Stephen John Stedman", *International Journal*, 64 (4), Autumn 2009, pp. 1160-1161.

66 Francis Mading Deng (1996), *Sovereignty as Responsibility: Conflict Management in Africa*, Washington D.C.: Brookings Institution Press.

67 Ibid.

68 Ibid.

69 Francis Deng, "Idealism and Realism: Negotiating Sovereignty in Divided Nations", *The 2010 Dag Hammarskjöld Lecture*, Uppsala University, 10 September 2010, http://www.un.org/en/preventgenocide/adviser/pdf/DH_Lecture_2010.pdf

70 Ibid.

71 Ibid.

72 Francis M. Deng, Interview, Question & Answer Session on Darfur, *The Washington Post*, August 14, 2004.

73 Ibid.

Chapter -2

Conflict Resolution in Africa: AU's Commitment

The African Union has larger mandate to help resolve inter-state and intra-state conflicts, deal with theorist threats and engage in peace-building exercises. The AU Charter has equipped the member states better in terms of handling conflict related problems through collective action. Accordingly, Article 3(f) of its Constitutive Act states that one of the AU's aims is to 'promote peace, security and stability.' In addition, Article 4 (e) states that one of the AU's principles is the 'peaceful resolution of conflicts among member states.' The AU legitimately and frequently deploys its Pan-African troopers in the conflict theatres. The AU has over the years successfully focused its commitment towards prevention, containment and resolution of armed conflicts in Africa.

This chapter has evaluated AU's commitment in prevention, containment and resolution of intertwinedly linked intra and inter-state armed conflicts in Africa. It has looked at AU's involvement in dealing with crises in Darfur and Somalia, given the sustained nature of armed conflicts in these two cases.

African State System

The genesis of African state system lies in the historicity of post-colonial state formation. The state was born in Europe and then exported to the rest of the world by colonial powers, notably Britain, France and Spain. As Opello and Rosow write, "It is impossible to understand the modern states without taking into account the way European states constructed an interconnected global order by means of conquest, trade, religious conversion and diplomacy."[1] Thus the state was super imposed on ethnic, regional and religious divisions that had themselves been strengthened by the rigid classifications of the colonialists.[2]

Characterising the post-colonial state in Africa, Davidson suggests that it has proved to be the 'black man's burden' rather than 'Europe's last gift' to the continent.[3] The boundaries of half of its sates contain at least one straight section and many national borders are treated with indifference by governments and people alike. Some are completely unguarded, hardly the sign of a state concerned to demonstrate its territorial mastery.[4]

Conversely, Elliott Green maintained that African states are both unusually large and well known for having artificial borders created during the colonial period. While African state size and shape have been previously shown to be correlated with negative development outcomes, he showed that African state size and shape are not arbitrary but are rather a consequence of Africa's low pre-colonial population density, whereby low-density areas were consolidated into unusually large colonial states with artificial borders. He also explained that state size has a strong negative relationship with pre-colonial trade and that trade and population density alone explain the majority of the variation in African state size. Finally, he rules out a relationship between population density and state size or shape among non-African former colonies, thereby emphasizing the distinctiveness of modern African state formation.[5]

Sabelo J. Ndlovu-Gatsheni again deploys the concept of 'coloniality of power' to critically reflect on the decolonisation process, using a 'colonial difference' perspective which enables a critical reflection on the limits of decolonisation from the side of the ex-colonised ordinary citizens of Africa. Three principal arguments are advanced. First, celebration of the decolonisation process as the proudest moment in African history obscures the continuing operation of the colonial matrices of power in maintaining Africa's subaltern position in global politics. Second, decolonisation resulted only in politico-juridical freedom, which is often conflated with freedom for the ordinary peoples of Africa. Third, celebrations of decolonisation are belied by the fact that ordinary African citizens engaged in new struggles for freedom soon after decolonisation aimed at liberating themselves from oppression by the inherited and imposed post-colonial African state.[6]

Sabelo delves into the genealogical, ideological and ethical elements of decolonisation, alongside its political assumptions and implications. This facilitates the decoupling of ideas of liberation from notions of emancipation, which are often considered the same thing. It also enables critical engagement with the character of the post-colonial African state imposed on Africans without being fully reconstituted and decolonized institutionally. A fresh appreciation of ordinary citizens' ongoing struggles for liberation from the postcolonial state, exemplified by the current North African popular uprisings against dictatorial regimes, is provided.[7]

He further interrogates the African postcolonial condition with a focus on the thematics of liberation predicament and the long standing crisis of dependence (epistemological, cultural, economic, and political) created by colonialism and coloniality. A sophisticated deployment of historical, philosophical, and political knowledge in combination with the equi-primordial concepts of coloniality of power, coloniality of being, and coloniality of knowledge yields a comprehensive and truly refreshing understanding of African realities of sub-alternity. How global imperial designs and coloniality of power shaped the architecture of African social formations and disciplined the social forces towards a convoluted 'postcolonial neo-colonized' paralysis dominated by myths of decolonization and illusions of freedom emerges poignantly in his analysis.[8]

What distinguishes his study is its de-colonial entry that enables a critical examination of the grammar of decolonization that is often wrongly conflated with that of emancipation; bold engagement with the intractable question of what and who is an African; systematic explication of the role of coloniality in sustaining Euro-American hegemony; and unmasking of how the 'postcolonial' is interlocked with the 'neo-colonial' paradoxically. It is within this context that the postcolonial African state emerges as a leviathan, and the 'postcolonial' reality becomes a terrain of contradictions mediated by the logic of violence. His theoretical arguments are buttressed by the detailed empirical case studies of South Africa, Zimbabwe, DRC and Namibia.[9]

He tries to explicate the role of colonialism of power (a global neo-colonial hegemonic model of power that articulates race and labour, as well as space and people in accordance with the needs of capital and to the benefit of white European people) in shaping the complex history of the African postcolonial present. According to him, it is a 'present' which is 'absent' because what exists is not what Africans aspired for and struggled to achieve. Africans and other peoples of the Global South who experienced 'darker' manifestations of modernity which included such processes as the slave trade, mercantilism, imperialism, colonialism and apartheid, aspired for a new humanity in which species of the human race would coexist as equal and free beings. African nationalism and decolonization were thus ranged against all the dark aspects of modernity, including underdevelopment and epistemic violence. But what emerged from the decolonization process was not a new world dominated by new humanist values of freedom, equality, social justice and ethical coexistence. African people found themselves engulfed by a 'postcolonial neo-colonized world' characterized by myths of decolonization and illusions of freedom.[10]

The term 'postcolonial neo-colonized world' best captures the difficulties and unlikelihood of a fully decolonized African world that is free from the snares of the colonial matrix of power and the dictates of the rapacious global power. The current configuration of the world is symbolized by the figure of America at the apex and that of Africa at the bottom of the racialized and capitalist hierarchies, of a world order. Such dark aspects of European modernity as the slave trade, mercantilism, imperialism, colonialism and apartheid bequeathed to Africa a convoluted situation within which the 'postcolonial' became paradoxically entangled with the 'neo-colonial', to the extent that the two cannot be intellectually approached as mutually exclusive states of being.[11]

In short, the term 'postcolonial neo-colonized world' captures a normalized abnormality whereby issues of African identity formation, nation-building and state-construction, knowledge production, economic development and democratization remained unfinished projects mainly because of their entrapment within colonial matrices of modern global power. African leaders are also entrapped within a disciplining colonial matrix of power and those who try to deviate and question the commandment from the powerful Euro-American world are subjected to severe punishments and in extreme cases even assassinations. Therefore, within the context of a 'postcolonial neo-colonized world' such issues as identity formation, nationalism, decolonization, nation building, liberal democracy, epistemology and economic development form a single part of a complex discursive formation whose genealogy is traceable to the underside of modernity and so cannot be treated separately if a clear and broader picture of the African postcolonial present is to be understood.[12]

African Security Environment

The seemingly enduring nature of African security problems and the various attempts to resolve them have been constant features of the post-colonial period, shaping relations among African states, their societies and the international community.[13] At the heart of this situation is the condition of the African state and its weaknesses, variously diagnosed as rooted in the structural legacies of colonialism and neo-colonial practices, and a fundamental disjuncture between an elitist state and diverse societies, or suffering from deficiencies ranging from deep-seated corruption to chronic policy mismanagement.[14]

While the notion of constructing a sustainable state apparatus featured to a degree in the independence struggle and colonial rationalisations for maintaining suzenrainty, this debate was largely abandoned in favour of a swift withdrawal of formal European control in most of Africa. The phenomena of "juridical sovereignty" and the rise of "shadow states" and a host of other pathologies affecting the African state diagnosed by Western academics in the wake of independence were exacerbated by clientalist practices, the appropriation of the state for personal gain and the devastating impact of structural adjustment policies aimed at resolving these dilemmas. As a result, throughout much of this period African security was conceived and addressed by independence leaders whose focus was on strategies aimed at dismantling colonial rule, engaging in post-colonial nation-building that was primarily given expression through the strengthening of authoritarian rule, and finding ways of accommodating foreign influence that were mostly framed in the terms of the exigencies of the cold war.

With the ending of the cold war and the concurrent onset of a democratisation process across the continent, starting in Benin in 1991 and winding its way across much of Africa, a new security agenda for the continent began to take shape. It was primarily oriented towards managing these potentially volatile transitions away from authoritarianism and conflict and, as such, emphasised peacekeeping and the building of liberal institutions. This was formalised through the UN secretary general's Agenda for Peace (1992; amended 1995) and reflected influential initiatives of the day such as the Commonwealth's Commission on Global Governance.[15] African leaders, led by Salim Salim at the Organisation for African Unity (OAU), attempted to revitalise the regional approach to security on the continent in the early

1990s, laying the basis of many of the normative changes through the Conference on Security, Stability, Development and Cooperation in Africa.[16]

A turning point in the African security debate was finally reached with the massive failure of the international community and its African partners to stem the tide of instability, destruction and genocide in countries such as Somalia, Rwanda, Liberia and the Democratic Republic of the Congo (DRC). These "new wars", said to be motivated by "greed and grievance", exposed the severe deficiencies of some African states in managing complex claims to legitimacy and the effective allocation of national resources – deficiencies variously rooted in ethnicity, chronic deprivation and administrative corruption or failure.[17] The result was to spur on an expanded discourse that diagnosed the sources of African insecurity as rooted in governance failures and aimed to address these through a range of policy prescriptions that included external intervention on humanitarian grounds and built on past precedents of the comprehensive restructuring of the continent's economic and governance institutions. Collectively characterised as "liberal peace" and given expression through processes that led to the UN Summit on the Responsibility to Protect and the establishment of the Commission on Peacebuilding in 2005, these plans were realised in UN-sanctioned interventions in the DRC and Sudan.[18]

For Africa, these enhanced efforts at tackling security were integrated into the tranformation of the OAU into the AU, a process that culminated in 2002 with the passage of the Constitutive Act. The African Peace and Security Architecture (APSA) that emerged from this process was a five-pronged system composed of the Peace and Security Council (PSC), the Early Warning System (EWS), the African Standby Force (ASF), the Panel of the Wise, the Peace Fund and the eight designated regional economic communities (RECs) – although only five presently lead in this area. The RECs – the building blocks of a possible continental union – have begun to develop regional forms of the ASF and EWS.[19] Notably, the AU provisions for intervention as described in Article 4 went well beyond the OAU's defensive posture on sovereignty to one predicated on "non-indifference", calling outright for intervention in cases of genocide, ethnic cleansing and other forms of conflict where the state had abrogated its responsibilities to its citizens.[20] Coupled to this was a more robust endorsement of peacebuilding, democratic governance and institutional development through the issuing of the Common African Defence and Security Policy in 2004 and the Declaration on Unconstitutional Changes of Government in 2009.[21] The AU, unlike its predecessor, has demonstrated a willingness to be actively involved in continental security issues, having suspended nine member governments for constitutional violations, applied sanctions against six member governments and authorised several peace support operations in the last decade.[22]

Nonetheless, relations between the AU and the RECs are widely seen to be "imbalanced" and unclear, with some well-developed regional organisations like the Economic Community of West African States (ECOWAS) able to field strong peace support missions, while others are effectively dysfunctional in terms of security matters.[23] Overall dependency on some key bilateral and multilateral partners, notably the European Union (EU) and UN, is evident: while African ownership of the APSA process is emphasised throughout, measured in financial terms this position is currently mostly rhetorical because Western governments supply the bulk of the financial requirements (98 per cent) of the operational components of the AU.[24] Particular peacekeeping operations, such as the AU/UN Hybrid Operation in Darfur (UNAMID), have relied almost exclusively on funding support from EU sources.[25] Moreover, the promotion of formalised ties between the UN Security Council and the AU – the only such regional arrangement and one strongly driven by South Africa during its two-term tenure as a non-permanent member of the Security Council –ensures that both African security issues and AU involvement feature high on the global agenda. Finally, important security issues, such as the continuing spread of arms sales – still dominated by the Western armaments industry and its Russian counterpart, although Chinese small arms are making an impact[26]– remain largely outside of official processes of scrutiny.[27]

Despite these changes to formal policy and greater international activism, improvements in African security still remain distressingly episodic, with regional leadership seen in peace support operations in West African conflicts and UN involvement limited to selective involvement in peacekeeping and monitoring operations in Somalia, the DRC and the Sudans. Given the low levels of development in Africa, which is characterised by states saddled with spiralling debt burdens that are incapable of providing domestic revenue and channelling investment into the public sector, and a foreign investment community that rarely looks beyond the extractive sector, the dire conditions in Africa seem fixed in a cycle of insecurity.[28]

African Peace and Security Architecture

Following its formal inauguration in Durban, South Africa, in 2002, the African Union (AU) has embarked on an elaborate normative and institutional transformation. These changes are meant to consolidate the gains from the anti-colonial struggle while carving a new path for the continent in the 21st century; a century that some have referred to as Africa's century. There is however consensus that the 21st century can only be Africa's century if the lingering security and socio-economic challenges on the continent are confronted in a holistic and deliberate manner. It is against this background that the AU instituted normative and institutional measures to tackle the myriad of conflicts that have impeded the continent's full realization of its potential. The irony is not lost on many on the continent today that despite being one of the richest continents in terms of natural resources, it has remained at the bottom of the development ladder; A development that could change if current economic growth trends on the continent are sustained.[29]

The adoption of the Constitutive Act, which established the AU, marked a radical shift in Africa's international relations. Article 4(h) and (j) of the Constitutive Act broke new ground by empowering AU member states to intervene in situations involving crimes against humanity, war crimes and genocide. The shift from non-intervention to what is now commonly referred to as non-indifference was largely informed by the genocide in Rwanda in 1994. The genocide in that country demonstrated two things; the absence of a normative and legal basis to intervene, and perhaps more crucially, the lack of capacity to do so, even if the legal hurdles were circumvented. Driven by the "never again" principle, the AU dispensed with the old rules that had governed inter-African relations, especially with respect to intervention in the internal affairs of its members. It embraced the principle of non-indifference, a more proactive norm, which if implemented would ensure that the terrible crimes committed in Rwanda in 1994 would never be repeated anywhere on the continent.[30]

In furtherance of its normative shift, the AU adopted the Protocol relating to the establishment of the Peace and Security Council (PSC), which entered into force on 26 December, 2003. The Protocol embraces an expanded and comprehensive agenda for peace and security that includes conflict prevention, early warning and preventive diplomacy, peace-making and peace building, the encouragement and promotion of democratic practices, intervention, humanitarian action and disaster management. The

Protocol elaborated a far-reaching African Peace and Security Architecture (APSA). The APSA is intended to give the AU the necessary instruments to fulfil the tasks set out in the Constitutive Act and the Protocol establishing the PSC.[31]

The Peace and Security Council (PSC) was established as the nerve centre of the APSA and to serve as a standing decision making Organ of the AU. It is to be supported by the AU Commission, the Panel of the Wise, the Continental Early Warning System (CEWS), an African Standby Force (ASF) and a Special Fund. The functions of these as mandated in the Protocol underscore the importance of interdependence and synergy between and among the pillars. The RECs/RMs are the building blocs of the APSA. Hence, there is also a parallel process of setting up functioning systems in the RECs/RMs. Consequently, the success of the APSA is therefore largely contingent on a synergistic linkage between the various ASPA components at one level, and the AU and the RECs/RMs at another.[32]

Article 12 of the Protocol provides for early warning information provided to the Chairperson of the Commission through the CEWS. This is meant to provide the PSC with an opportunity of taking the required action after due consideration of the issues. For its part, the Panel of the Wise could be deployed to support efforts of the Peace and Security Council (Article 11). In situations of grave magnitude as envisaged in Articles 4 (h) and (j) of the Constitutive Act, it could trigger some form of intervention. Hence, an African Standby Force is to be established to deal with such eventualities (Article 13). The Protocol envisages an inter-locking peace and security architecture that would address pressing security challenges on the continent. Thus, ensuring synergistic and coherent approaches would determine the success of the APSA in the medium to long-term.[33]

Regional Conflict Resolution Approach

Since the early 1990s, the resolution of intra-state conflicts and the improvement of domestic governance are treated as integral components to the successful implementation of regional agendas in Africa.[34] The engagement of the RECs and the AU into these areas proceeds from an attempt to redress and overcome what Hentz, Söderbaum and Tavares have described as the "Africa Paradox": while African states are committed to cede sovereignty to regional organizations, many of the substantive components of sovereignty elude them.[35]

The outcome is regional organizations that still aspire to the creation of security communities – the experience of the North Atlantic community[36] acts as the model of choice – yet must focus on the treatment of violence and insecurity within their member states. As observed in the introduction to *Routledge Handbook of African Security*, insecurity in Africa remains primarily driven by domestic violence and its knock-on effects across borders.[37] Conflicts over the delimitation of African boundary-lines are the exception, despite ongoing perceptions that the arbitrary establishment of most of these undermines their legitimacy. As a result of this specific context, the security dilemma of the RECs revolves around a difficult balancing act between their aspiration to enforce intrusive agendas and the propensity of the member-states concerned to confine such interventionism to the legitimation of the status quo and the enforcement of regime stability.

This security conundrum was highlighted throughout 2012 by the complex negotiations that repeatedly delayed plans towards the deployment of a UN backed ECOWAS military force in Mali. Helping to restore the authority of the Malian state over the Islamists' dominated northern part of the country required the prior clarification that this would not result in an international legitimation of the coup staged in March 2012 by the military junta in Bamako – the chaos that ensued contributed decisively to the Islamists' and Tuaregs' successful takeover bid in the North. Under the pressure of international sanctions, the Bamako junta eventually had had to concede the establishment of a government of national unity on 22 August 2012. As the ECOWAS head of States announced on 11 November 2012 their adoption of an integrated programme towards the deployment of an Africa-led international force, they acknowledged "the lead role of Mali" but simultaneously cautioned that military and diplomatic initiatives would seek to restore constitutional order, as well as the unity and territorial integrity of the country. The linchpin of the "two-pronged" approach adopted by the ECOWAS was the commitment of the Interim President of Mali to announce shortly a roadmap towards the organization of free, fair and transparent elections.[38]

For a number of ailing regional economic groupings, institution-building in the field of security has also opened avenues for the enhancement of their resources and legitimacy. In Central Africa a largely formal economic grouping, ECCAS has undertaken, since 2002, to carve a new role for itself in the world of conflict prevention and peace-keeping. In the Horn, the

Intergovernmental Authority on Drought and Development (IGADD), now known as IGAD, has carved a niche for itself as a forum and an interface for UN, EU and US sponsored initiatives over Somalia, the Sudan and the conflict between Eritrea and Ethiopia. In both cases, policymaking at regional level heavily reflects upon politics within member-states and their ability to produce public policies, not least with respect to the conception of security as a common good. The African state, as Aning's chapter stresses in this volume, keeps providing the prism through which African security, including within a regional context, is best understood.[39]

Until the early 1990s such notions as rule of law, good governance and security were conspicuously absent from the mandates of Africa's regional and sub-regional organizations that were originally expected to focus exclusively on economic integration. This chapter traces the overall evolution of regionalism in Africa, from its initial emphasis on regional economic integration to its current focus on regional security. The following chapters in the book, after taking a closer look at the African Union, will then discuss the Economic Community of West African States (ECOWAS), the Southern African Development Community (SADC), the Inter-Governmental Authority on Development (IGAD) and the Economic Community Central African States (ECCAS).

Promoting collective self-reliance provided the initial rationale for regional economic integration in Sub-Sahara Africa, as symbolized by the commitments of the Lagos Plan of Action (1980) and Abuja Treaty (1991) to an African Economic Community. The related implementation of import-substitution policies within African states was grounded in the widespread perception among rulers, scholars, government officials, and experts that African states were trapped in a dependent relationship with the industrialized North. Furthermore, and most importantly, that relationship was considered to be both inherently unequal and self-perpetuating. Breaking the ties that bound African states to their ex-metropoles was depicted as sine qua non to economic development, especially due to trade relations that typically involved exporting primary products in return for manufactured goods.

Little progress towards regional economic cooperation – not to mention integration – has been achieved since those early days. Nonetheless, the mandate of regional economic cooperation schemes from the Economic Community of West African States (ECOWAS) to the Southern African Development Community (SADC), has expanded to include regional security as well as economic cooperation. Many of the roadblocks that limited progress towards regional economic cooperation have been reinterpreted, more broadly, as the expression of governance and security problems.

The common association of regional integration with transferring components of sovereignty, as occurred in Europe, to a supranational entity, also cuts across the grain of post-colonial African politics. Until the end of the cold war period, most African states were ruled by authoritarian military or single party regimes that would reject any constraints on the enhancement of the power and personal wealth of incumbent rulers. Non-interference into the internal affairs of member-states provided the overarching framework to which both regional organizations and the Organization of African Unity (OAU) had to abide. Post-colonial patronage linkages and cold war alignments also, and most importantly, offered alternatives to raising regional security issues within sub-regional groupings. These were deeply divided, due to conflicting interpretations of what security should entail among member states: emphasis on non-intervention into the domestic affairs of member-states went along with the de facto treatment of security as a no go area.[40]

Two decade later, Africa's eight Regional Economic Communities (RECs) and the AU draw much of their legitimacy and the vast majority of their resources from their aspiring role as peace-keepers and agencies of restraint. The regional implications of violence and disregard for the rule of law within member-states are no longer minimized or overlooked. The contagion effects of unstable conflict-ridden states in Africa are no longer underestimated. Conflict can easily cross Africa's permeable borders, as exemplified by the Liberian conflict, the DRC conflict, and the Darfur conflict. Region-building in Africa, therefore, has become mostly and overtly focused on state (re)construction and sovereignty enhancement.[41]

The redeployment of Africa's RECs and the AU into the field of peace and security contrasts sharply with the disappointing track record of these same inter-governmental organizations (IGOs) when it comes to their original mandate and stated goals, namely the promotion of economic integration, so as to ultimately promote a pan-African market. After a discussion of what has been termed new regionalism, it is necessary to look at the evolution of regionalism from its original economic focus towards holistic agendas, which treat regional security and governance as priorities.[42]

African Standby Force

Article 13 of the Protocol Establishing the Peace and Security Council of the African Union envisages the establishment of an African Standby Force (ASF). The ASF is an integral component of the African Peace and Security Architecture and will play a critical function in enabling the PSC to fulfil its mandate. The ASF is organized into five regional standby forces, previously known as regional brigades. The formation of the regional forces includes a full time Planning Element (PLANELM); a Logistics Depot (LD); a Brigade Headquarters; and the Pledged Brigade Units. The various RECs and RMs are at various stages of establishing the aforementioned structures, although some regions like SADC have opted not to establish a standing Brigade Headquarters.[43]

There have been contentious discussions about membership of the ASF regional groupings. Ideally, the Regional Economic Communities could have been used as the formation for the ASF regional brigade. However, there are currently eight RECs and the ASF is designed on the basis of 5 regions. As a result there are some Member States that belong to more than one regional brigade. Therefore, the use of RECs as organisational units of the ASF brigades has turned out to be challenging. However, the five regional groupings are tentatively divided as follows:[44]

The Southern African Grouping known as the Southern Africa Standby Force (SASF) includes: Botswana, Lesotho, Malawi, Mozambique, Namibia, South Africa, Swaziland, Tanzania, Zambia, and Zimbabwe. Angola and the Democratic Republic of the Congo (DRC) also belong to the Central Grouping. Madagascar and Mauritius are also members of this group. The Eastern Africa Grouping known as the Eastern Africa Standby Force (EASF) is composed of Burundi, Comoros, Djibouti, Eritrea, Ethiopia, Kenya, Sudan, Rwanda, Seychelles, Somalia, and Uganda. The Central African Grouping known as the Central African Standby Force (CASF) is composed of Burundi, Cameroon, Central African Republic, Chad, Congo-Brazzaville, Equatorial Guinea, and Sao Tome Principe. Angola and the DRC could potentially belong to the Southern Grouping. The West Africa Grouping known as the ECOWAS Standby Force (ESF) is composed of Benin, Burkina Faso, Cape Verde, Côte d'Ivoire, Gambia, Ghana, Guinea-Bissau, Liberia, Sierra Leone, Mali, Niger, Nigeria, and Senegal.[45]

The North African Grouping known as the North African Regional Capability (NARC) is composed of Algeria, Egypt, Libya, Mauritania, Tunisia and Western Sahara. However, this brigade is yet to make the expected progress. According to the 2003 Policy Framework for the Establishment of the ASF and the Military Staff Committee (MSC) and the 2005 Roadmap for the operationalisation of the ASF, subsequently supplemented by Roadmap II, the ASF was to be developed in two phases and inaugurated in 2010. At the end of Phase II in 2010, the ASF was supposed to be operationally ready for deployment including for complex peacekeeping operations and intervention in response to grave circumstances – war crimes, crimes against humanity and genocide – as defined under Article 4 (h) of the Constitutive Act of the AU. However, following the AMANI Africa Exercise, the ASF was assessed to have reached only its Initial Operational Capability (IOC), Roadmap III was then developed to support the Full Operational Capability (FOC) of the ASF by 2015.[46]

However, even if the ASF is fully operationalized by 2015, there are still some more practical issues relating to the adoption of the Draft AU decision making process/aide-Memoire already used during the Amani Africa Exercise for absence of a coherent policy with regard to mandating and coordination of the ASF. In addition, the AU is working for a specific legal framework, within the APSA, for the establishment and use of the ASF before its FOC by 2015. This will help to clarify the key function of the PSC and other institutions of a similar nature at the RECs level. The AU's technical competence also has to be enhanced, and issues such as the Rapid Deployment Capability (RDC) and logistical infrastructure, including the establishment of the Regional Logistic Base (RLB) in Douala, Cameroon, of the ASF have to be in place to enable the activation of Regional Brigades for future ASF missions.[47]

The PSC communiqué PSC/PR/BR (CLXVI) issued on 16 January 2009, 'commended the Commission for the activities undertaken within Roadmap II' and more specifically 'welcomed the efforts deployed and the progress made towards the full operationalisation of Regional Brigades, the implementation of the ASF Training Plan through the initialisation conference of the AMANI Africa Exercise and the Rapid Deployment Capability'. Additionally, the PSC requested the Commission 'to undertake further work to implement the ASF Policy Documents' and 'to develop and finalise the additional documents and submit proposals on those areas to Ministers of

Defence and Security, for their early action towards the implementation of the ASF by 2010.'[48]

After the PSC adopted the communiqué, the AU submitted a report in May 2009 on progress made at the 6th Meeting of African Chiefs of Defence Staff (ACDS) and Heads of Safety and Security, which followed the Experts Meeting of ACDS. The Declaration adopted by the African Chiefs of Defence Staff and Heads of Safety and Security noted 'the ongoing efforts to improve upon the Rapid Deployment Capability Concept, the Continental Logistics Bases (CLBs), work on the Strategic Lift Capability Concept, the Formed Police Unit (FPU) Concept, development of the Civilian Dimension and the elaboration of an ASF Training Plan 2009 – 2010, as well as the various training efforts'. The Experts Meeting noted that a key challenge was the 'lack of common understanding between the AUC and the RECs / RMs on mandating of missions'. This is an issue that results from the way the ASF was designed and is currently being operationalised.[49]

As conceptualised in the relevant ASF Policy documents and further institutionally developed, the ASF is a force organised into five Regional Brigades composed of multidisciplinary contingents on standby in their country of origin. The Brigades that together constitute the ASF are raised and maintained by the five Regional Economic Communities /Regional Mechanisms (ECOWAS, NARC, EASBRICOM, ECCAS, and SADC) which serve as building blocks of the Peace and Security Architecture of the AU. This structural organisation of the ASF suggests that there are at least two entities having authority over the use and deployment of the ASF: the AU and RECs/RMs.[50]

The ASF Policy Framework provides that each REC/RM will have to prepare, by 2010, a capability, consisting of military, police and civilians elements of about 5,000 personnel. This means that the overall size of the ASF will come to a capability of 25,000 – 30,000.[51] This has the potential to address aspects of the problem of force generation as ASF forces are pledged by states ahead of the decision for deployment. Even in this regard however, a lot depends on the establishment of the necessary legal arrangements between the AU and RECs, between RECs/RMs and member states as well as the adoption of the necessary laws at the national level. Without the necessary legal instruments, the AU would still need to negotiate individually with member states for the release of their pledged contingents. Without the necessary national laws as well, member states may face serious legal problems in releasing their pledged contingents, particularly in the case of sensitive AU missions.[52]

Efforts to operationalize the ASF has registered good progress although, the degree of progress varies from region to region. Progress in developing a multidimensional concept for the ASF is perhaps one of the most remarkable to date. The Military and Police components have been put in place in all RECs and RMs. However, there are still some crucial gaps, especially as it relates to the civilian component. The absence of a binding framework between the AU, RECs/RMs and their member states is a critical gap that should be addressed as matter of urgency. Meanwhile, the AU should adopt an advocacy plan to raise awareness about the ASF. It is hoped that lessons from the 2010 AMANI exercise and practical experience from the AU's peace operations in Darfur (AMIS and UNAMID) and Somalia (AMISOM) would contribute to achieving Full Operational Capability (FOC) by 2015.[53]

African Court of Human Rights and Justice

The AU Constitutive Act provided for an African Court of Justice to be established as one of the AU's principal organs. The Protocol of the Court was adopted in July 2003.[54] However, the Court did not become operational. The AU Assembly decided at its July 2008 Summit to merge the African Court of Justice and Human Rights with the African Court on Human and Peoples' Rights (see previous entry) into an African Court of Justice and Human Rights.[55]

The Assembly adopted the 2008 Protocol on the Statute of the African Court of Justice to merge the courts (Assembly/AU/Dec.196 (XI)). Article 28 of the 2008 Protocol provides that the African Court of Justice and Human Rights shall have jurisdiction over all cases and legal disputes that relate to "the interpretation and application of the Constitutive Act, Union treaties and all subsidiary legal instruments, the African Charter and any question of international law".[56]

In June 2014, the Assembly adopted a further Protocol on Amendments to the Protocol on the Statute of the African Court of Justice and Human Rights (Assembly/AU/Dec.529(XXIII)). Transition to the new Court will begin after 15 Member States have ratified the 2008 Protocol on the Statute of the African Court of Justice and Human Rights. As at September 2014, 30 states had signed the 2008 Protocol (most recently Madagascar on 31 January 2014) and five had ratified it (most recently Benin on 28 June 2012).[57]

The adoption of the Protocol on the Statute of the African Court of Justice and Human Rights ("the new Protocol") by the Assembly of the African Union completes the process of establishing a new Court, which is considered the main judicial organ of the African Union.[58] The new Protocol replaces two previous protocols, the Protocol to the African Charter on Human and Peoples' Rights on the Establishment of an African Court ("the 1998 Protocol")[59] and Protocol of the Court of Justice of the African Union ("the 2003 Protocol").[60] Given the increased emphasis on human rights and democratization in Africa since the late 1990s, the main reason for the 1998 Protocol under the African Charter on Human and Peoples' Rights[61] (1981) was to enhance and strengthen the protective mandate of the African Commission on Human and Peoples' Rights, which, in spite of improvements to the Commission's individual complaint mechanism, remains quite weak.[62]

The 2003 Protocol was adopted pursuant to Article 18 of the Constitutive Act of the African Union ("the Act"). The broader objectives of the African Union, as compared to those of the Organization of African Unity, and the fact that the Court of Justice is the only judicial organ referred to in the Act, are both indicators that the new Court was conceived to have jurisdiction over various issues covered in the Act, including disputes relating to questions of international law and the interpretation and application of the Act, and other treaties and instruments adopted within the framework of the African Union.[63]

In July 2004, the Assembly of the African Union decided to merge the African Court of Human and Peoples' Rights and the Court of Justice of the African Union,[64] following a proposal by the Chairperson of the Assembly of the African Union, President Olusegun Obasanjo. The decision was based on concerns regarding the increasing number of African Union institutions and the cost of maintaining them. The main idea was to consolidate the limited resources available for a single court. In January 2005, the Commission of the African Union recommended that the necessary amendments to both the 1998 and 2003 Protocol be made, and that these amendments become effective through adoption of a new protocol by the Member States. This proposal would have required that the African Court of Human and Peoples' Rights (ACHPR) begin operation (since the 1998 Protocol had entered into force) before the ratification process for the Protocol on the Court of Justice was finalized, a side effect that would have necessitated a later integration of the two courts. However, in July 2005, the Assembly ultimately decided that the merger should be realized through the adoption of a single legal instrument.[65] At the Eleventh Summit of the African Union, which took place between June and July 2008, the Assembly adopted the new Protocol, which gave effect to the Assembly's July 2005 decision.[66]

The new Protocol provides that the Constitutive Act of the African Union be read in reference to the African Court of Justice and Human Rights (ACJHR).[67] Concerns had been expressed regarding the potential overlap in jurisdiction ratione materiae of the ACHPR and the Court of Justice of the African Union. This was addressed by dividing the new Court into two Sections, namely a General Affairs Section and a Human Rights Section, both composed of eight judges. The General Section is competent to hear all cases, except those "concerning human and/or peoples' rights", which are reserved for the Human Rights Section.[68] The qualifications of judges, who are elected to each Section, differ accordingly. Furthermore, each Section may decide to refer a case to the Full Court for consideration.

The new Protocol also provides that the 1998 Protocol will remain in force for up to one year after the entry into force of the new Protocol, in order to enable the ACHPR to take the necessary measures pertaining to the transfer of its prerogatives, assets, rights and obligations.[69] The current members of the ACHPR were elected in 2006 and will remain in office until the election of the new ACJHR judges. Cases pending before the court will be transferred to the Human Rights Section of the new Court. This will allay concerns that the merger will interfere with the momentum behind the ACHPR.[70]

The relationship between the African Commission on Human and Peoples' Rights and the ACHPR has also been the subject of discussion, and the need to address this relationship in that Court's Rules of Procedure has now been transferred to the ACJHR. Article 38 of the Statute provides that the Rules of Court take into account "the complementarity between the Court and other treaty bodies of the Union."[71]

Regarding jurisdiction ratione personae, States Parties to the new Protocol, organs of the African Union, and staff members of the Union may submit a case to the Court in accordance with the Staff Rules and Regulations (Article 29 of the Statute). In human rights cases, the new Protocol preserves a much noted feature of the 1998 Protocol, which allows that actions be brought before the Court not only on the basis of the African Charter on Human Rights and the related Protocol on the Rights of Women in Africa, or the Charter on the Rights of the Welfare of the Child, but also on the basis of any instrument that has been ratified by a State Party to the new Protocol (Article 30). The ACJHR thus has the potential of becoming a venue for adjudicating numerous international violations, including human rights, humanitarian law and other subjects "relevant to human rights". However, in spite of demands by several non-governmental organizations for direct access to the Court by individuals, the new Protocol preserves the 1998 Protocol requirement that Member States expressly declare that they accept the competence of the Court to receive cases brought by individuals and accredited non-governmental organizations.[72]

This may be viewed as a retrograde development, given that the sub-regional courts in Africa (such as the Court of Justice of the Economic Community of West African States, the Court of Justice of the Common Market of the East and Southern Africa, the Southern African Development Community Tribunal, the East African Court of Justice, and the Court of Justice of the Economic and Monetary Union of West Africa) all allow individuals direct access. Nevertheless, in principle, if States do issue such declarations accepting jurisdiction, and if the African Union is liberal in accrediting NGOs, this could prove to be an important provision.[73]

According to Article 46 of the new Protocol, the ACJHR "shall" refer cases of non-compliance with its judgments to the Assembly of the African Union, which shall decide what measures it will take to impose sanctions. While this is an important improvement regarding enforcement of the African Commission on Human and Peoples' Rights' decisions, the Assembly's approach with respect to enforcement remains to be seen.[74]

The creation of a pan-African court of general competence is significant, especially since several sub-regional courts exist that could form a system of courts with the single African court created by the new Protocol at its apex. Regarding human rights, it will be interesting to see how the Human Rights Section of the ACJHR develops the African Charter on Human and Peoples' Rights, including its provisions for third generation human rights (or rights of solidarity) and its unique emphasis on the duties of the individual.[75]

UN-AU Security Interface

In terrain of Africa, as elsewhere in the world, the aim of the host of multilateral initiatives on peace and security is to tackle the root causes of conflict by embarking on socio-political and economic transformation through the promotion of democracy and market liberalism,[76] an ambition that set them apart from previous UN operations.[77] In 1992, the UN Secretary General laid out the framework for this deeper form of international engagement in post-conflict states, defining peacebuilding as far "more than the reconstruction of the peace after the cessation of hostilities."[78] The launching of the Brahimi Report eight years later paved the way for reform of the UN approach to peace operations that included a diagnosis of the root causes of conflict in poverty and a prescription for its solution through the promotion of "sustainable development and a democratic society with respect for human rights." The report also called for a more substantive role for the UN in peacebuilding.[79] In turn, this led to the establishment of the UN Peacebuilding Commission in 2005 with its mandate for selective international intervention.[80] The Peacebuilding Commission received further attention with the 2011 World Development Report on "Conflict, Peace and Development" and the concomitant work of the OECD-DAC group on "fragile states."[81]

At the same time that international policy debates on peacebuilding were moving closer to the formal institutionalization of practices, there was a concurrent interest in Western and African scholarly and policymaking circles in rendering state sovereignty conditional on responsible governance, and expanding the scope for humanitarian intervention.[82] A Canadian-sponsored commission on intervention and state sovereignty was created in 2000 and, coupled to the African Union's (AU) strong endorsement of humanitarian intervention in its constitutive act in 2002, laid the foundation for the 2005 UN World Summit and Responsibility to Protect (R2P). Taken together, all these developments in the first decade of the 21st century contributed to what came to be characterized as the canon of "liberal peacebuilding" and dominated international approaches to handling the complexities of state reconstruction, economic rehabilitation and encouraging societal peace in the aftermath of war.[83]

Both the United Nations (UN) Security Council and the Peace and Security Council (PSC) of the African Union (AU) have a vested interest in conducting more effective peace operations in Africa. Both councils want to build on the various UN-AU peace and security coordination mechanisms that have been established since 2006 and support the implementation of the AU's principle of "non-indifference." In many respects, considerable progress has been made with the UN and AU enjoying a deep, multidimensional and maturing relationship. Yet disagreements remain over how best to respond to particular peace and security challenges in Africa, and the AU still suffers from important capability gaps with respect to peace operations.[84]

It is necessary to analyze the evolution of collaboration between the two councils on peace operations and asks how the institutions can cooperate more effectively in this area. After providing an overview of UN-AU collaboration on peace and security issues in general and peace operations in particular, one has to observe the AU Mission in Somalia as a crucial case that exemplifies some of the positive and negative aspects of the UN-AU relationship. There are some of the ongoing challenges that will need to be overcome if the two councils are to optimize their collaboration and deploy legitimate and effective peace operations. There is scope for offering some practical recommendations for enhancing UN-AU relations in this area.[85]

The central challenges blocking more effective AU-UN collaboration on peace operations can be identified across three dimensions: the strategic, political relationship between the two councils; the bureaucratic and organizational interaction between the two councils; and intra-AU dynamics, namely, relations among the AU Commission, the Peace and Security Council, and AU member states. One may offer practical recommendations designed to address each of these dimensions by the following: a) harmonizing the decision-making processes of the two councils; b) filling some of the key capability gaps in the AU's representation in New York; and c) developing more efficient communication mechanisms between the elected African members of the UN Security Council and the AU's Peace and Security Council in Addis Ababa.[86]

It is important to reiterate, however, that the essence of the relationship between the two councils and their members is political. Consequently, no amount of institutional reconfiguration will completely dispel the political frictions that are bound to occur when controversial issues and crises are discussed. There is an unavoidable trade-off between creating new mechanisms, enhancing the capabilities of existing institutional structures, and providing flexible arrangements which are nimble enough to adapt to unforeseen and rapidly evolving peace and security challenges.[87]

The build-up of a special relationship between the EU Commission and the African Union (AU) Commission dates back to the adoption of the AU's Constitutive Act in 2000. The EU Commission was not indifferent to a reform of the pan-African Organisation of African Unity (OAU) Charter that, at least formally, borrowed extensively from the EU (Bach-1, 2008).4 The African Union's new acronym (AU) was an explicit reference to the model of the EU. The Secretariat of the former OAU was to be known as the Commission, while the former Secretary-General of the OAU became President of the new Commission. There was also a Permanent Representatives' Committee that echoed the EU's Committee of Permanent Representatives or Comité des Représentants Permanents (Coreper). Regional disparities among AU members were also to be addressed through the creation of a Community, Solidarity, Development and Compensation Fund, an instrument evocative of the EU's structural funds. In the areas of peace-keeping and security, although the United Nations (UN) Security Council provided the template for the institutional structure of the AU's Peace and Security Council (PSC), its functions and objectives were meant to be integrated within a Common African Defence and Security Policy (CADSP) that intimated a parallel with the EU's Common Security and Defence Policy (CSDP).[88]

More important than this somewhat formal emulation of the European model was the spectacular departure of the AU Constitutive Act from the OAU Charter's past emphasis on strict non-interference in the domestic affairs of member states.[89] The Constitutive Act of the AU prescribed the establishment of an African peace and security architecture that would uphold 'the right of the Union to intervene in a Member State pursuant to a decision of the Assembly in respect of grave circumstances, namely war crimes, genocide, and crimes against humanity' — Article 4 (h) (AU, 2000). The signatories also condemned and rejected 'impunity and political assassination, acts of terrorism, and subversive activities' — Article 4 (o) — along with 'unconstitutional changes of government' — Article 4 (p). Article 30 also prescribed that the AU had the right to suspend the membership of any government that violated these principles.[90]

The assertion of these principles went along with a readiness of the undertake new responsibilities, a move that dovetailed with the reluctance of the United States (US) and the EU to commit troops to UN peace-keeping operations since the Somalia and Rwanda disasters. This convergence boosted the adoption of a European policy of constructive disengagement aimed at promoting Africa-led operations and capacity-building in the areas of good governance, conflict prevention, and peace-keeping. At least initially, European engagement into short term peace-keeping missions in Africa was viewed as an opportunity to test the objectives assigned to the CSDP, after the crisis in the Balkans had dramatically highlighted Europe's weaknesses in the field of conflict prevention.

For the European Commission, providing financial, staff and logistical support to the AU and its peacekeeping missions also created opportunities to expand the reach of first-pillar (Community) activities through peace and security missions that had a clear link with development objectives. In an area that used to be the exclusive preserve of EU member states (through the CSDP), the European Commission was now also able to craft and develop autonomous policies. Accordingly, substantial financial support for peace-support operations had been channelled to the AU by the EU Commission through the establishment of a specific financial instrument, the African Peace Facility (APF). Endowed with 250mn drawn from the European Development Fund, the APF has contributed to transform the EU into the largest funding partner of the AU.[91]

The rationale for constructive disengagement has also meant that whenever the direct intervention of European troops in Africa was agreed upon — for example, in 2003, when Operation Artemis was launched in the Democratic Republic of Congo (DRC); in 2006, when the European Union Force (Eufor) was sent to the DRC; and in 2007, with the deployment of Eufor in Chad and the Central African Republic — this has been on a short-term basis and with the explicit objective to prepare a handover to UN troops. Such processes have also been associated with increased coordination or 'Europeanisation' of the policies of EU member states.

UNAMID

A civil war which broke out in 2003 led to the deaths of tens if not hundreds of thousands of Darfuris and the displacement of nearly two million. In the fighting between the Government of Sudan and militias and other armed rebel groups, widespread atrocities such as the murder and rape of civilians have been committed. The UN raised the alarm on the crisis in Darfur in 2003, and finding a lasting resolution has been a top priority for the Security Council and two consecutive Secretaries-General. Under the auspices of the African Union (AU) and with support of the UN and other partners, the

Darfur Peace Agreement (DPA) was signed on 5 May 2006. As few parties signed on, a renewed peace process under a joint AU-UN mediator took place in Doha, Qatar, over 2010 through June 2011, producing a framework document. Intensive diplomatic and political efforts to bring the non-signatories into agreement with the Doha Document for Peace in Darfur continue.[92]

Following the 16 November 2006 High-Level consultations in Addis Ababa, Ethiopia, the UN Department of Peacekeeping Operations (DPKO) augmented the existing African Union Mission in Sudan (AMIS) and prepared to deploy an unprecedented joint AU/UN peacekeeping operation in Darfur. Intensive diplomacy by Secretary-General Ban Ki-moon and several actors in the international community resulted in Sudan's acceptance of this force in June 2007. The African Union/UN hybrid operation in Darfur was formally established by the Security Council on 31 July 2007 through the adoption of resolution 1769, referred to by its acronym UNAMID, under Chapter VII of the UN Charter. UNAMID formally took over from AMIS on 31 December 2007.

The mandate is renewed yearly, and the adoption of Security Council resolution 2173 on 26 August 2014 extended it for a further 10 months, until 30 June 2015. The Mission's headquarters is in El Fasher, North Darfur. It has sector headquarters in El Geneina (West Darfur), Nyala (South Darfur), Zalingei (Central Darfur) and El Daein (East Darfur). The Mission has 35 deployment locations throughout the five Darfur states. On 31 July 2007, the Mission had an authorized strength of 25,987 uniformed peacekeepers. This included 19,555 troops, 360 military observers and liaison officers, 3,772 police advisers and 2,660 formed police units (FPU). In mid-2011, UNAMID stood at 90 per cent of its full authorized strength, making it one of the largest UN peacekeeping operations.[93]

By resolution 2063 of 31 July 2012, the Security Council decided to decrease strength of military and police components. The Mission has now an authorized strength of 23,743 personnel. This includes up to 19,248 uniformed peacekeepers (15,845 troops, 1,583 police advisers and 1,820 formed police units) and a civilian component of up to 4,495 peacekeepers (1,185 international staff, 340 UN volunteers, and 2,970 national personnel).[94]

The budget of UNAMID was US$ 1.29 billion for the fiscal year 2013 - 2014. UNAMID is confronted with numerous logistical and security constraints as it must operate in unforgiving terrain and in a complex and often hostile political environment. The Mission also faces shortfalls in critical transport, equipment, infrastructure and aviation assets. In the meantime, UNAMID is doing all in its power and with limited resources to provide protection to civilians in Darfur, facilitate the humanitarian aid operation, and help provide an environment in which peace can take root. The mission carries out more than 100 patrols daily. UNAMID also works to address some of the critical roots of the conflict.

UNAMID's work is complemented by joint efforts on the political front. Until mid-2008, the Joint Mediation Support Team was led by the UN Secretary-General's Special Envoy for Darfur, Jan Eliasson, and the AU Special Envoy for Darfur, Salim Ahmed Salim. On 30 June 2008, UN Secretary-General Ban Ki-moon and AU Commission Chairperson Jean Ping appointed Djibril Yipènè Bassolé, the Foreign Minister of Burkina Faso, as the new joint AU-UN Chief Mediator for Darfur. As of 8 June 2011, Mr. Bassolé returned to Burkina Faso, and Ibrahim Gambari, Joint Special Representative (JSR) of UNAMID, became the Joint Chief Mediator ad interim. On 1 August 2012, UNAMID Deputy JSR (Political), Aichatou Mindaoudou, succeeded Mr. Gambari as Joint Chief Mediator a.i. On 20 December 2013, UN Secretary-General Ban Ki-moon and AU Commission Chairperson Nkosazana Dlamini-Zuma, appointed Mohamed Ibn Chambas of Ghana as UNAMID's JSR and UN - AU Joint Chief Mediator.[95] Thus, UNAMID is a useful case study of AU's involvement in conflict resolution process in Darfur. African Union Mission in Somalia (AMISOM) is a similar case in point.

AMISOM

Given the sustained nature of armed conflicts in Somalia, the African Union Mission in Somalia (AMISOM) experiment, involving regional and global actors, has added to its success story on the security front. Nevertheless, the AU has further scope to improve upon its pre-emptive security efforts which would avert the West Gate kind incident in the future. The AMISOM is an active, regional peace-keeping mission operated by the AU with the approval of the UN. The UNSC in its latest resolution passed on March 6, 2013 declared to maintain deployment of the AMISOM until February 28, 2014. It was created by the AU's Peace and Security Council on January19, 2007 with an initial six month mandate. AMISOM replaced and subsumed the IGAD Peace Support Mission to Somalia (IGASOM), which was a proposed Inter-Governmental Authority on Development (IGAD) protection and training mission in Somalia approved by the AU in September 2006. IGASOM was also approved by the UNSC.

Dr. Nkosazana Dlamini-Zuma, Chairperson of the Commission of the African Union (AU), condemned the colossal terrorist attacks on September 21, 2013 against non-combatant civilians in West Gate Shopping Mall in the Kenyan capital Nairobi, causing massive human casualty. The Chairperson of the Commission stated that the cowardly attack, for which the al Qaeda-linked Al Shabaab group claimed responsibility, once again underlined the imperative for renewed and reinvigorated efforts to combat terrorism throughout the continent. She reiterated the AU's commitment to continue working with its member states and partners to this end. She expressed the solidarity of the AU with the government and peoples of Kenya. The Chairperson of the Commission reiterated the AU's commitment to sustain its efforts to counter terrorism throughout the continent, as well as to pursue its efforts to stabilize the situation in Somalia and the fight against Al Shabaab, through the AMISOM.[96]

Similarly, AU's Deputy Chairman Erastus Mwecha said the fight against terrorism will not be discontinued in spite of the attack. Mwecha stated, "Of course, today its Kenya, tomorrow it would be elsewhere, so we must continue to fight, and that is why the need for international cooperation is absolutely important....We've indicated our resolve to continue to fight terrorism in whatever form it exists. We are also aware that this is a global menace and we need to act together as the international community to fight the scourge." He mentioned that the AU is working with its international partners to assist Kenya following the terrorist attack. Mwecha added, "But, we are also encouraged to see that a number of member states have already given their support and willing to assist Kenya." Sharing condolences to the victims' families and hailing the Kenyan government for of its manner of handling the crisis, he noted, "For now, we wait to see [if] the Kenya authorities give us [an] assessment of the extent of the needs, and the African Union will then respond accordingly."[97]

Claiming responsibility for the attacks, Al Shabab stated the attack was in response to Kenya's military action in neighboring Somalia. Kenya had sent troops into Somalia in October 2011 following a series of terror attacks on Kenyan territory said to have been carried out by forces operating out of Somalia. The United Nations Security Council (UNSC), which partly finances the six-year-old AMISOM operation, approved Kenya's participation in the 17,000-member force in a resolution adopted in February 2011.

Subsequently, a total of 4,664 Kenyan security personnel deployed in Somalia were formally integrated into AMISOM's ranks. To this effect, the Kenyan Government and the AU Commission signed a Memorandum of Understanding at the AU headquarters in Addis Ababa on June 2, 2012. The AU Commissioner for Peace and Security Amb. Ramtane Lamamra commended Nairobi for its demonstrated commitment and continued support to AMISOM and noted that Kenya's entry into Somalia in October 2011 was a significant game changer to the efforts towards bringing normalcy in Somalia. In September 2012, the Kenyan forces captured the strategic port city of Kismayu, which was their strategic target and the key source of funding for the Al-Shabaab militia. In June 2013, veteran Al-Shabab leader Sheikh Hassan Dahir Aweys was taken into custody by government troops after he is ousted by more extreme Al-Shabab figure Ahmed Abdi Godane. In September 2013, international donors promised 2.4 billion dollars in reconstruction aid in three-year 'New Deal.'[98]

There was, however, spike in violence with various attacks by Al-Shabab, including on presidential palace and UN compound in Mogadishu. Al-Shabab carried out series of attacks in Kenya. In September 2013, Al-Shabab seized shopping centre and killed 60 people in Kenyan capital Nairobi, saying it is retaliation for Kenya's military involvement in Somalia. In May 2014, Al-Shabab says it carried out a bomb attack on a restaurant in Djibouti, saying the country is used as a launch pad to strike Muslims. In June 2014, Al-Shabab claimed two attacks on the Kenyan coast which killed more than 60, saying operations against Kenya would continue.

In September 2014, Al-Shabab leader Ahmed Abdi Godane was killed in US drone strike. Government offered 2 million dollar bounty for his successor, Ahmad Omar. In November-December 2014, Al-Shabab carried out mass killings in north-east Kenya, including on a bus and a camp of quarry workers. In April 2015, Al-Shabab claimed responsibility for killing 148 people, mainly Christian students, at Garissa University College in northern Kenya. Kenya carried out air raids on Al-Shabab bases in Somalia in retaliation.

Endnotes

1   Walter C. Opello and Stephen J. Rosow (2004), *The Nation-State and Global Order: A Historical Introduction to Contemporary Politics*, Boulder, CO and London: Lynne Rienner, P. 161.

2   Rod Hague and Martin Harrop (1982), *Comparative Government and Politics: An Introduction*, Hampshire and New York: Palgrave Macmillan, pp. 29-30.

3   Basil Davidson (1992), *The Black Man's Burden: Africa and the Curse of the Nation-State*, Oxford and Harare: James Currey, p.188.

4   Op.cit, Hague and Harrop, p.32.

5   Elliott Green, "On the Size and Shape of African States", *International Studies Quarterly*, 56 (2), June 2012, p. 229.

6   Sabelo J. Ndlovu-Gatsheni, "Fiftieth Anniversary of Decolonisation in Africa: A Moment of Celebration or Critical Reflection? *Third World Quarterly*, 33 (1), 2012, p. 71.

7   Ibid.

8   Sabelo J. Ndlovu-Gatsheni, (2013), *Coloniality of Power in Postcolonial Africa: Myths of Decolonization*, Dakar: CODESRIA.

9   Ibid.

10   Ibid, p. x

11   Ibid, p. xi

12   Ibid.

13   Chris Alden, "Seeking Security in Africa: China's Evolving Approach to the African Peace and Security Architecture", Norwegian Peacebuilding Resource Centre, Report March 2014, http://www.peacebuilding.no/var/ezflow_site/storage/original/application/357f0f6e29c92422ce98ce152a9e4819.pdf

14   For an overview of this topic, see Williams, Paul. (2011), *War and Conflict in Africa*, Cambridge: Polity Press.

15   CGG (Commission on Global Governance). 1995. Our Global Neighbourhood. Oxford: Oxford University., pp.77-112.

16 Jeng, Abou. 2012. Peacebuilding in the African Union: Law, Philosophy and Practice. Cambridge: Cambridge University Press, p.157.

17 Kaldor, Mary. 1999. *New Wars and Old Wars*. Stanford: Stanford University Press.; Collier, Paul & Anika Hoeffler. 1999. *Greed and Grievance in Civil Wars*. World Bank Report. Washington, DC: World Bank.

18 Paris, Roland. 2004. *At War's End: Building Peace after Civil Conflict*. Cambridge: Cambridge University Press.

19 AU (African Union). 2010. African Peace and Security Architecture (APSA): 2010 Assessment Study. Report commissioned by the AU Peace and Security Department. Zanzibar, Tanzania, November.:p.8.

20 AU (African Union). 2000. Constitutive Act of the African Union. Addis Ababa: AU.

21 Vines, Alex. 2013. "A decade of African Peace and Security Architecture." *International Affairs*, 89(1), pp. 90-91.

22 Ibid., pp. 91-93.

23 Vorrath, Judith. 2012. "Imbalances in the African Peace and Security Architecture." *SW Comments*, 29, September: 1-2.; AU (African Union). 2010. *African Peace and Security Architecture (APSA): 2010 Assessment Study*. Report commissioned by the AU Peace and Security Department. Zanzibar, Tanzania, November.

24 Vorrath, Judith. 2012. "Imbalances in the African Peace and Security Architecture." *SW Comments*, 29, September: 1-2.

25 Engel, Ulf & Joao Porto. 2010. "Africa's new Peace and Security Architecture: an introduction." In Ulf Engel & Joao Gomes Porto, eds. *Africa's New Peace and Security Architecture: Promoting Norms, Institutionalising Solutions*. Farnham: Ashgate., p. 4.

26 Bromely, Mark, Matheiu Duchatel & Paul Holtom. 2013. "China's exports of small arms and light weapons." SIPRI Policy Paper no. 2013:38. Stockholm: SIPRI, pp. 41-47.

27 Op.cit., Chris Alden.

28 Ibid.

29 Alhaji Sarjoh Bah, Elizabeth Choge-Nyangoro,Solomon Dersso, Brenda Mofya and Tim Murithi (2014), "African Peace and Security Architecture: A Handbook," Addis Ababa: Friedrich-Ebert-Stiftung (FES)/AU, p. 16.

30 Ibid.

31 Ibid, 17.

32 Ibid.

33 Ibid, 18.

34 Daniel C. Bach (2013), "Regionalism in Africa: Concepts and Context", in James J. Hentz (Ed.) *Routledge Handbook of African Security*, London: Routledge

35 Fredrik Söderbaum, Rodrigo Tavares and James Hentz, "Regional Organizations and African Security: Moving the Debate Forward", *African Security*, 2 (2-3), p. 214.

36 Deutsch, 1957

37 James J. Hentz (Ed.) (2013), *Routledge Handbook of African Security*, London: Routledge.

38 ECOWAS 2012

39 Daniel C. Bach (2013), op.cit.

40 Bach 1983

41 Daniel C. Bach (2013), op.cit.

42 Ibid.

43 Alhaji Sarjoh Bah et al, op.cit., p. 50.

44 Ibid.

45 Ibid, p.51-52.

46 Ibid, 52.

47 Ibid.

48 Ibid.

49 Ibid, 52.

50 Ibid, 53.

51 This will rise to about 40,000 following the decision of the May 2009 ACDS and Heads of Security Meeting to increase the police standby arrangement from the 240 Individual Police Officers (IPOs) per REC/RM to 720 and the FPU from 2 to 6 per REC/RM. See Johan Potgieter Peacekeeping Forces for Peace Support Operations in Africa ISS Today (4 August 2009) available on www.issafrica.org.

52 Alhaji Sarjoh Bah et al, op.cit., p. 54.

53 Ibid.

54 The 2003 Protocol on the African Court of Justice entered into force in February 2009, 30 days after 15 Member States had ratified it. As at 1 September 2014, 44 Member States had signed the Protocol (most recently South Sudan on 24 January 2013) and 16 had ratified it (most recently Gambia on 30 April 2009).

55 African Union Hand Book 2015, http://www.au.int/en/sites/default/files/MFA-AU-Handbook-2014-ENGLISH-v17%20interactive%281%29_0.pdf, p. 92.

56 Ibid.

57 Ibid, p. 93.

58 Protocol on the Statute of the African Court of Justice and Human Rights, art. 2, available at http://www.hurisa.org.za/Advocacy/AfricanCourt/Single_Legal_Instument.pdf [herein after New Protocol].

59 Protocol to the African Charter on Human and Peoples' Rights on the Establishment of an African Court, adopted on June 10, 1998, entered into force January 25, 2004, OAU Doc.OAU/LEG/EXP/AFCHPR/PROT(III), available at http://www.oecd.org/dataoecd/42/47/38963691.pdf. The Draft Protocol, which was adopted unmodified, is reprinted in 9 Afr. J. Int'l & Comp. L. 953 (1997).

60 Protocol of the Court of Justice of the African Union, July 11, 2003, reprinted in 13 Afr. J. Int'l & Comp. L. 115 (2005).

61 African Charter on Human and Peoples' Rights, adopted June 27, 1981, OAU Doc. CAB/LEG/67/3/Rev. 5, reprinted in 21 LL.M. 58 (1982), entered into force October 21, 1986.

62 The Commission is a quasi-judicial body without the power to make binding decisions. Its functions are limited to examining state reports, considering

communications alleging violations, and interpreting the Charter. See, e.g., G. M. Wachira & A. Ayinla, Twenty Years of Elusive Enforcement of the Recommendations of the African Commission on Human and People 's Rights: A Possible Remedy, 6 Afr. Hum. Rts. L.J. 465 (2006).

63 Olufemi Elias, "Introductory Note to the Protocol on the Statute of the African Court of Justice and Human Rights", *International Legal Materials*, 48 (2), 2009, p. 334.

64 Decisions on the Seats of the African Union, Assembly/AU/Dec. 45 (III), f 4, adopted July 6-8, 2004.

65 Decision on the Merger of the African Court on Human and Peoples' Rights and the Court of Justice of the African Union, Assembly/AU/Dec. 83 (V), adopted July 4-5, 2005. The decision expressed the Assembly's gratitude for the offer of the Minister for Foreign Affairs of Algeria and former President of the International Court of Justice, Mohammed Bedjaoui, to contribute to the drafting of the new Protocol.

66 Decision on the Single Legal Instrument on the Merger of the African Court on Human and Peoples' Rights and the African Court of Justice, Assembly/AU/ Dec. 196 (XI) June 30-July 1, 2008.

67 New Protocol supra note 1, art. 3. See N. Udombana, An African Human Rights Court and an African Court: A Needful Duality or A Needless Duplication?, 28 Brook. J. Int'l L. 811 (2002-2003) (arguing for the merger).

68 Statute of the African Court of Justice and Human Rights, arts. 16 & 17.

69 New Protocol, supra note 1, art 7. Protocol of the Court of Justice of the African Union, art. 60 (provides for its entry into force after ratification by fifteen Member States. The fifteenth instrument of ratification was deposited by Algeria in January 2008).

70 Op.cit. Olufemi Elias, p.335.

71 See, e.g., Ibrahim Ali Badawi El-Sheikh, *The Future Relationship between the African Court and the African Commission*, 2 Afr Hum. Rts. L.J. 252 (2002).

72 Op.cit. Olufemi Elias, p.335.

73 Ibid.

74 Ibid.

75   Ibid.

76   Chris Alden and Daniel Large, "On Becoming a Norms Maker: Chinese Foreign Policy, Norms Evolution and the Challenges of Security in Africa", *The China Quarterly*, 2015, p.6.

77   Berdal, Mats. 2009. *Building Peace after War*. London: The International Institute for Strategic Studies.

78   See Boutros-Ghali 1992.

79   25 United Nations press release SC/6948, 4220th meeting, 13 November 2000, http://www.un.org/press/en/2000/20001113.sc6948.doc.html.

80   High Level Panel on Threats. 2004. "A more secure world – our shared responsibility." Report to the United Nations, New York, http://www.un.org/en/events/pastevents/a_more_secure_world.shtml. Accessed 14 January 2015, especially paragraphs 221–230.

81   World Bank. 2011. World Development Report 2011: Conflict, Security, and Development, http:// siteresources.worldbank.org/INTWDRS/Resources/WDR2011_Full_Text.pdf. Washington, DC: World Bank.

82   See Deng, Francis M., Sadikiel Kimaro, Terrence Lyons, Donald Rothchild and I. William Zartman. 1996. *Sovereignty as Responsibility: Conflict Management in Africa*. Washington, DC: The Brookings Institution.

83   Mayall, James, and Ricardo Soares de Oliveira (eds). 2011. *The New Protectorates: International Tutelage and the Making of Liberal States*. London: Hurst.

84   Arthur Boutellis and Paul D. Williams, "Peace Operations, the African Union, and the United Nations: Toward More Effective Partnerships", IPI, April 2013 http://reliefweb.int/sites/reliefweb.int/files/resources/Peace%20Operations,%20the%20African%20Union,%20and%20the%20United%20Nations%20Toward%20More%20Effective%20Partnerships.pdf

85   Ibid.

86   Ibid.

87   Ibid.

88   Daniel Bach, "The European Union and Africa: Trade Liberalisation, onstructive Disengagement, and the Securitisation of Europe's External Frontiers", *Africa Review*, 3 (1), 2011: p.41

89 Magliveras & Naldi, 2009

90 AU, 2000

91 Vines & Middleton, 2008

92 UNAMID,http://unamid.unmissions.org/Default.aspx?tabid=10998&
    language=en-US

93 Ibid.

94 Ibid.

95 Ibid.

96 IANS, "African countries condemn Kenya mall attack", September 25, 2013

97 Ibid.

98 BBC News, Somalia Profile – Timeline, http://www.bbc.com/news/world-
    africa-14094632

Chapter – 3

Political Stability in Africa: AU's Mandate

The African Union (AU) has accorded a prominent position to political democracy by recognizing its credibility as an 'enabling choice system' that fosters economic growth and stability in Africa. The AU's commitment to democracy is demonstrated by its significant role as an effective moderator in competitive claims over electoral mandates in the African countries, which nurture the strong quest for their democratic entitlements. Constraining the consolidation of procedural democracy in these politically 'aspirational and polarized' countries, the constant electoral contestation is cumulatively caused and compounded by a multiplicity of factors. These include, *inter alia*, arbitrary territorial demarcation by the colonial powers, Cold War encampments of the super powers, externally imposed multi-party system, ethno-centric political dispensation, competition between traditional (Western) and emerging extra-regional powers for economic space, and the use of political dissent as strategic opportunity by the Western actors in Africa.

This chapter has examined AU's capacity as a moderator in competitive claims over juridical and electoral mandates in the African countries which are in the quest for their democratic entitlements. It has studies the 2013 election in Zimbabwe and the 2011 regime change in Libya to assess AU's political stability mandate in Africa.

Neopatrimonialism in Africa

There is a striking contrast between the dissemination of the concept of neopatrimonial rule in Africa and its more parsimonious mobilization outside the continent. The increasing assimilation of the African neopatrimonial state to integral and predatory forms of politics has contributed to its perception as a global prototype of the 'anti-developmental' state.[1] The concept of neopatrimonial rule was first applied to Africa in the late 1970s, when Jean-Franc,ois Me´dard sought to account for the Cameroonian state's lack of institutionalisation and 'underdevelopment'.[2] Cameroon, he noted, is simultaneously a 'strong, authoritarian, absolute . . . and impotent' state, where political-administrative authority is converted into a private patrimony by a bureaucracy and a party closely controlled by President Ahidjo.[3] The lack of distinction between office and officeholder, Me´dard went on, is masked behind discourses, juridical norms and institutions that nourish the illusion of a legal-bureaucratic logic. The distinction between public domain and private interest is, in practice, 'negated and made to lose any substance'.[4] In the absence of a legitimizing ideology, the ruler owes his ability to remain in power to his capacity for transforming his monopolistic control over the state into a source of opportunities for family, friends and clients.

Neopatrimonialism in Africa is still classically viewed as the outcome of a confusion between office and officeholder within a state endowed, at least formally, with modern institutions and bureaucratic procedures. The introduction of 'neo' as a prefix also means that neopatrimonialism is freed from the historical configurations with which patrimonialism had been associated by Weber.[5] The display of legal-bureaucratic norms and structures coexists with relations of authority based on interpersonal rather than impersonal interactions:

As with classic patrimonialism, the right to rule is ascribed to a person rather than to an office. In contemporary neopatrimonialism, relationships of loyalty and dependency pervade a formal political and administrative system and leaders occupy bureaucratic offices less to perform public service than to acquire personal wealth and status. The distinction between private and public interests is purposely personal favours, both within the state . . . and in society . . . [6]

The concept of neopatrimonialism, due to the coexistence of patrimonialism with legal-bureaucratic elements, begs the question of the forms of interaction and their outcomes. Indeed, neopatrimonialism infers a 'dualistic situation, in which the state is characterised by patrimonialisation, as well as by bureaucratisation'.[7] The concept, similarly conclude Bratton and van deWalle, refers to situations where the 'patrimonial logic coexists with the development of bureaucratic administration and at least the pretence of legal-rational forms of state legitimacy'.[8] Such dualism can effectively translate into a wide array of empirical situations. These mirror variations in the state's failure or capacity to produce 'public' policies.

Me'dard, who had grown increasingly aware of the conceptual drift caused by undifferentiated descriptions of neopatrimonialism, sketched, in the late 1990s, a taxonomy based on the mode and intensity of the regulation of patrimonial practices. His suggestion was to identify 'two types of African states representing two polar points, with all possible intermediate situations: at one end of the spectrum, neopatrimonial states characterised by a patrimonial mode of political regulation based on redistribution (Coˆte d'Ivoire under Houphoue¨t-Boigny), and, at the other end, purely predatory states that correspond to a sultanic type of patrimonialism (Mobutu's Zaı¨re)'.[9] In the following pages, we argue that political systems where patrimonial practices tend to be regulated and capped should be distinguished from those where the patrimonialisation of the state has become all-encompassing, with the consequent loss of any sense of public space or public policy.

Regulated Neopatrimonialism

In Africa, regulated forms of neopatrimonialism have been usually associated with the introduction of a policy of ethnoregional balance. The distribution resources and prebends by the ruler is sometimes formalised and can take place on an inclusive base. The emphasis laid on cooptation and redistribution, rather than coercion, contributes to promote a culture of mutual accommodation. The expected outcome is an increased state capacity to penetrate society and ensure compliance. Even though notions as public ethics and common good may be undercut, regulated neopatrimonialism conveys its own brand of 'moral economy', in so far as it favours redistribution processes that target the national territory.[10]

The regimes of Jomo Kenyatta (1964–1978) and Fe'lix Houphoue¨t-Boigny (1960–1993) offer good examples of regulated neopatrimonialism. Kenyatta's attempt to reconcile contradictory imperatives has also been described as a case of 'rationalised clientelism'. Within the Kenyan bureaucratic state, argues Daniel Bourmaud, impersonal rules were made to co-exist with neopatrimonial practices designed to alleviate the risks that political competition might carry for the Nation-State.[11] Synergies between presidentialism, single-party system and what amounted to an institutionalized system of patronage facilitated the incorporation of the periphery by the centre.

In Cote d'Ivoire, the regime of Fe´lix Houphoue¨t-Boigny (1960–1993) similarly exemplified the combination of personal rule with regulated neopatrimonialism. The trademark of Houphoue¨t, a prototype of the 'big man' in politics,[12] was his capacity to combine intra-elite cooptation with limited usage of coercion. Direct control was exerted over the recruitment of the political elite so as 'to balance ethnic, generational and even personal rivalries'.[13] The outcome was a hybrid political system where 'strong personal power . . . through patron-client relations [combined with] the use of modern bureaucratic agencies'. Patrimonial interference in the bureaucratic activities of the state was restricted.[14] The country's political and administrative elites appear, observed Richard Crook in the late 1980s, far less divided than in the 'patrimonial bureaucracies' of other African states. Patrimonial elements within the political system, 'have . . . not been allowed to override the commitment set from the top to legal-rational forms of control, effective role performance and the implementation of an economic programme'.[15] The pursuit of regulated practices over a relatively long period also invited to draw parallels with the country's remarkable political stability. In practice, this meant that the imprint of neopatrimonialism was capped and ring fenced.

The 1960s and early 1970s were the golden ages of regulated neopatrimonialism in Africa. Commodity export revenues were still high and rulers could have access to significant resources to combine public policy implementation with the development of extensive patronage networks. Personal rule and the consolidation of single-party or military regimes did not necessarily appear incompatible with ensuring state- (if not nation-) building.[16]

Predatory Neopatrimonialism

Predatory forms of neopatrimonialism refer in Africa to systems where personal rule and resource control reach a paroxysmic level, with a consequent 'failure of institutionalisation .... and thus of the state'.[17] The corollaries are the absence of a public space, and of any capacity to produce 'public' policies. Indeed, the privatisation of the public sphere is carried to such extremes that it becomes conducive to its dissolution.[18] In the Central African Republic, under the Bokassa regime, desinstitutionalisation and the rise of informal practices eventually challenged the very notion of a state.[19]

It is the evolution of the Mobutu regime (1965–1997) after 1974 that seems to have offered the purest illustration of a thoroughly patrimonialised system. Mobutu's brand of neopatrimonial rule, observes René Lemarchand, differed from others on the continent due to an 'unparalleled capacity to institutionalize kleptocracy at every level of the social pyramid and his unrivalled talent for transforming personal rule into a cult and political clientelism into cronyism'.[20] Mobutu's 'predatory' rule, also noted Crawford Young and Thomas Turner, involved the permeation of the state by a level of corruption so pervasive as to have become its most visible and defining property.[21] Qualified as arbitrary, predatory or kleptocratic, Mobutu's Zaire has also called for parallels with sultanism – the term coined by Max Weber to characterise those extreme instances where the ruler's domination relies less upon traditional foundations than on the leader's arbitrary and uncontrolled power.[22]

Sultanism has also become commonly associated with the totalitarian and bloody exercise of power by Idi Amin in Uganda (1971–1979), Macı́as Nguema of Equatorial Guinea (1968–1979) and Jean Bedel Bokassa in Central Africa (1966–1979).[23] In Nigeria, Sani Abacha's rule (1983–1998) was treated as a case bordering on sultanism although the notion of 'predatory rule' was then preferred so as to avoid any risk of confusion with Nigeria's own sultanates.[24]

The distinction between regulated and predatory forms of neopatrimonialism signals the two extremes of a diversity of empirical configurations. In the case of integral and predatory forms of neopatrimonialism, the ruler exerts unrestrained control over the 'state'. The ultimate outcome of such a pattern may be the combination of kleptocracy with a narrowly defined distributive bias.[25] The very notion of a 'neopatrimonial state' becomes then an oxymoron. Conversely, regulated neopatrimonialism infers some capacity to craft 'public' policies but this may, over time, build-up into an increasingly 'legal-rational' modus operandi of the state. To put it differently, an operational distinction has to be drawn between patrimonial practices within the state and the patrimonialisation of the entire state.[26]

AU's Promotion of Governance and Development Norms

On issues relating to governance, the AU has sought to establish norms to guide the behaviour of its member states. In particular, the African Union Charter on Democracy, Elections and Governance is a seminal document, which has been ratified by the required fifteen member states and is accordingly a living document that outlines a range of provisions on how countries can improve their governance. The challenge is to ensure that these norms are actually adopted and implemented.[27]

African countries have consistently expressed their desire to regain control of their economic development policies, in order to improve their citizens' access to education and health care. The Structural Adjustment Programmes (SAPs) and so-called Poverty Reduction Strategy Papers (PRSPs) promoted and enforced by the International Monetary Fund (IMF) and World Bank have had a negative impact on development. Both the IMF and the Bank have admitted that these programmes did not achieve the desired results, while the United Nations Conference on Trade and Development (UNCTAD) estimates that IMF/World Bank policies led to a 10 percent decline in economic growth in Africa.[28]

The AU's New Partnership for Africa's Development (NEPAD) should be understood in this context. NEPAD was conceived as the means to enable Africa to accelerate its active participation on equal terms in the international economic sphere, and was endorsed by the Group of Eight (G8) in June 2002.[29] The key objectives of NEPAD include developing a viable Pan-African market economy, through infrastructure development and the promotion of intra-African trade, as well as improved access to education, training, and healthcare.[30] NEPAD has now been fully integrated into the AU with a Coordinating Agency based at the Union's headquarters in Addis Ababa.

At the AU's Assembly in 2002, held in Durban, the Declaration on the Implementation of NEPAD was adopted. It included a more specific 'Declaration on Democracy, Political Economic and Corporate Governance', which also established the African Peer Review Mechanism (APRM). The objectives of the APRM are to enhance African ownership of its development and governance agenda, to identify, evaluate, and disseminate best practices, and to monitor progress towards agreed goals. Member states are invited to join the APRM to participate in a self-monitoring programme with a clear timeframe for achieving certain standards of inclusive governance, premised on a commitment to accountability through peer pressure. However, as with many good intentions, both NEPAD and the APRM have fallen short when it comes to implementation.[31]

The G8 (now the G20) have not lived up to the development promises that they made in 2002 in terms of approaching Africa as a partner rather than a patron, while critics of NEPAD argue that the programme cannot succeed because it tries to integrate Africa into a global framework of neo-liberal laissez-faire economics, which is part of the reason why the continent found itself in such a difficult economic position in the first place.[32] In addition, African governments have only paid lip service to the APRM, due to its intrusive approach to domestic governance issues.

African Governance Architecture

The transition from the OAU to the AU is based on the ideational shift from 'secretive' sovereignty to 'collective' sovereignty. The AU has, consequently, institutionalised African Peace and Security Architecture (APSA) and African Governance Architecture (AGA). While APSA concerns peace and security matter of the continent, AGA is the overall political and institutional framework for the promotion of good governance in Africa. Given the exclusive emphasis put on the APSA, there is now a realisation for creating synergies between the AGA and the APSA.[33]

The 16th Ordinary Session of the Assembly of Heads of State and Government of the African Union which convened in Jan. 2011 under the theme "Towards Greater Unity and Integration through Shared Values" adopted the AGA and its Platform by endorsing the: a) EC Decision EX .CL Dec. 619 (XVIII), b) Assembly/AU/Decl.1(XVI). The AGA is the overall political and institutional framework for the promotion of good governance in Africa by enhancing interaction and synergies between African Union organs/institutions with a formal mandate in governance and strengthen and their capacity to produce "Shared" agendas of Governance.[34]

In this context, the African Governance Platform as an informal setting is established to strengthen cooperation and coordination among AU organs/institutions and other stakeholders with a governance mandate. Guided by the adopted Rules of Procedure, it operates on cluster's basis. Members of the African Governance Platform are AfCHPR, PAP, AUCIL, APRM, AUABC, ECOSOCC, ACERWC, RECs, PRC and PSC. There are four clusters: a) Democracy, Elections and Governance, b) Public Service, Administration, Anti-Corruption, Decentralization and Local Governance, c) Human and Peoples' Rights and Transitional Justice, and d) Humanitarian Affairs.[35]

Guided by the AU Constitutive Act, and the African Charter on Democracy, Election and Governance, this cluster aims at monitoring the implementation of democratic electoral processes and standards in member states, monitoring the changes leading for good governance at the national level, develop a Reporting and an Implementation Framework for the domestication of the Charter, developing a Framework to accelerate the ratification and domestication of Shared Values Instruments, creating synergies between the AGA and the Peace and Security Architecture (APSA), and issuing an annual report on the state of democracy and governance in Africa titled "the African Union Governance Report" including an index on Election.[36]

Guided by the African Charter on the Values and Principles of Public Service and Administration, this Cluster aims at facilitating experience sharing on State modernization and transformation as well as public service delivery efforts in AU member states, monitor and evaluate the relevant instruments and the implementation of its Long Term Strategy by member states, develop a 'Member State Reporting Framework' on the implementation of relevant instruments and issue an annual index on the "State of Service Delivery" and an index on "Assets Recovery" an index on "the State of Decentralization and Local Governance" as part of the African Union Governance Report".[37]

Guided by the African Charter on Human and Peoples' Rights and other relevant instruments, the Cluster aims at coordinating with the concerned organs to monitor the promotion and protection of human and peoples' rights on the continent, monitoring the implementation of the Human Rights Strategy for Africa and its Action Plan, developing a framework to speed the ratification and domestication of continental and global Human Rights Instruments, coordinating the efforts to develop the Transitional Justice Policy Framework for Africa and issuing a "Human and Peoples' Rights Index" as part of the "the African Union Governance Report."[38]

Guided by the Convention Governing the Specific Aspect of Refugee Problem in Africa and the AU Convention for the Protection & Assistance to Internally Displaced Persons in Africa, Humanitarian Affairs Cluster aims at monitoring and evaluating the implementation of the provisions of the treaties, through the development of an appropriate mechanism, developing coherent mechanism for the implementation of durable solutions to situations of forced displacement, ensuring that the root causes of forced displacement are addressed by bringing to the attention of Member States the findings of governance reports on the causes of such situations, promoting the signature, ratification and ascension of the two treaties on forced displacement, encouraging the development of a common and convergence policy framework for free movement of persons, developing an appropriate continental guideline to facilitate interregional movement of persons, and issuing an annual index on the "State of Humanitarian Affairs in Africa" as part of the African Union Governance Report".[39]

Pan-African Parliament

The Pan-African Parliament (PAP) is one of the nine organs proposed in the 1991 Treaty Establishing the African Economic Community (Abuja Treaty). Its purpose, as set out in article 17 of the AU Constitutive Act, is "to ensure the full participation of African peoples in the development and economic integration of the continent". The Parliament is intended as a platform for people from all African states to be involved in discussions and decision-making on the problems and challenges facing the continent. The Parliament sits in Midrand, South Africa.[40]

While the long-term aim is for the Parliament to exercise full legislative powers, its current mandate is to exercise advisory and consultative powers. The Parliament has up to 250 members representing the 50 AU Member States that have ratified the Protocol establishing it (five members per Member State).1 Under rule 7 of the PAP Rules of Procedure, a parliamentarian's tenure of office begins on the date he or she is elected or designated as a Member of Parliament. A parliamentarian's term should correspond to his or her own national parliament term or any other deliberative organ that elected or designated the parliamentarian.[41]

The long-term aim is for the Parliament to hold direct elections by universal suffrage. The PAP's functions are set out in the 2001 Protocol to the Abuja Treaty relating to the Pan-African Parliament and in its Rules of Procedure. These include: a) facilitate effective implementation of the OAU/African Economic Community's (AEC's) policies and objectives and, ultimately, the AU, b) work towards the harmonisation or coordination of Member States' laws, c) make recommendations aimed at contributing to the attainment of the OAU/AEC's objectives and draw attention to the challenges facing the integration process in Africa as well as the strategies for dealing with them, d) request OAU/AEC officials to attend its sessions, produce documents or assist in the discharge of its duties, e) promote the OAU/AEC's programmes and objectives in Member States' constituencies, f) encourage good governance, transparency and accountability in Member

States, g) familiarise the peoples of Africa with the objectives and policies aimed at integrating the African continent within the framework of the AU's establishment, h) promote the coordination and harmonisation of policies, measures, programmes and activities of Africa's parliamentary forums.[42]

The PAP adopts its own Rules of Procedure. These include provisions governing its functions, powers, voting, organs, committees and caucuses. During its June 2014 Summit, the AU Assembly adopted the Protocol to the Constitutive Act of the African Union on the Pan-African Parliament (Assembly/AU/Dec.529(XXIII)). Similarly, the Executive Council also decided that the PAP may on its own make proposals on the subjects and areas on which it may submit or recommend draft Model Laws to the Assembly for its consideration and approval (EX.CL/Dec.835(XXV)).[43]

The PAP originated with the Abuja Treaty (1991), which called for the establishment of a parliament to ensure that the peoples of Africa are fully involved in the economic development and integration of the continent. The Sirte Declaration (1999) repeated the call for early establishment. The Protocol Establishing the Pan-African Parliament was adopted at the 2001 OAU Summit in Sirte, Libya. The Parliament's first session was held in March 2004. PAP representatives are elected by the legislatures of their Member State, rather than being elected directly by the people. In addition to the full Assembly of Parliament, the PAP has 10 permanent committees. Under rule 28 of the PAP's Rules of Procedure, the Parliament should meet at least twice in ordinary session within a one-year period. Parliamentary sessions can last for up to one month. Under rule 29, the PAP can meet in extraordinary session.[44]

50 AU member states have so far ratified the PAP Protocol. They are Algeria, Angola, Benin, Botswana, Burkina Faso, Burundi, Cameroon, Cabo Verde, Central African Republic, Chad, Congo, Côte d'Ivoire, DR Congo, Djibouti, Egypt, Equatorial Guinea, Ethiopia, Gabon, Gambia, Ghana, Guinea, Guinea Bissau, Kenya, Lesotho, Liberia, Libya, Madagascar, Malawi, Mali, Mauritania, Mauritius, Mozambique, Namibia, Niger, Nigeria, Rwanda, Sahrawi Republic, Senegal, Seychelles, Sierra Leone, Somalia, South Africa, Sudan, Swaziland, Togo, Tunisia, Uganda, UR of Tanzania, Zambia and Zimbabwe.[45]

The PAP has nine permanent committees and one ad hoc committee, all of which discuss thematic issues. Under rule 28 of the PAP Rules of

Procedure on ordinary sessions, the permanent committees meet twice a year (March and August) for statutory meetings. The permanent committees can meet more often during parliamentary sessions or for non-statutory meetings.

First, Committee on Education, Culture, Tourism and Human Resources considers issues concerned with the development of human resources in member states. It assists the Parliament with policy development and implementation of programmes on issues of access to education, promotion of culture and tourism, and human resource development.[46]

Second, Committee on Cooperation, International Relations and Conflict Resolution considers policy issues on international cooperation and international relations on behalf of the Parliament and AU. It also deals with conventions and protocols linking the Parliament with regional and international institutions. The Committee examines revisions of AU protocols and treaties and provides assistance to the Parliament in its conflict prevention and resolution efforts.

Third, Committee on Gender, Family, Youth and People with Disabilities considers issues relating to the promotion of gender equality and assists the Parliament to oversee the development of AU policies and activities relating to family, youth and people with disabilities.

Fourth, Committee on Monetary and Financial Affairs examines the Parliamentary budget draft estimates. It also examines the AU budget and makes recommendations. The Committee reports to the Parliament on any problems involved in the implementation of the annual AU and PAP budgets. It advises the Parliament on economic, monetary and investment policies.

Fifth, Committee on Trade, Customs and Immigration Matters deals with matters relating to the development of policy for cross-border, regional and continental concerns within the areas of trade (primarily external trade), customs and immigration. It assists the Parliament to oversee relevant organs or institutions and AU policies relating to trade.[47]

Sixth, Committee on Health, Labour and Social Affairs works to support the implementation of social development, labour and health policies and programmes throughout the AU, including through regional and international cooperation strategies.

Seventh, Committee on Transport, Industry, Communications, Energy, Science and Technology deals with the development of transport and communications infrastructure. It assists the Parliament to oversee the development and implementation of AU policies relating to transport, communication, energy, science and technology, and industry.

Eighth, Committee on Rules, Privileges and Discipline assists the Parliament Bureau to interpret and apply the PAP Rules of Procedure, as well as matters relating to privileges and discipline. It considers requests for 'waivers of immunity' submitted under the Rules of Procedure and examines cases of indiscipline. The Committee also considers proposals for amending the Rules of Procedure.

Ninth, Committee on Justice and Human Rights assists the Parliament in its role of harmonising and coordinating member states' laws. It advocates for respect within the AU of the principles of freedom, civil liberties, justice, human and peoples' rights, and fundamental rights.[48]

Tenth, Committee on Rural Economy, Agriculture, Natural Resources and Environment considers the development of common regional and continental policies in the agricultural sector. It provides assistance to the Parliament to oversee and promote the harmonisation of policies for rural and agricultural development as well as the AU's natural resources and environmental policies.

Under rule 83 of the Rules of Procedure, each region should form a regional caucus composed of its members. There are five caucuses: a) Central Africa, b) Eastern Africa, c) Northern Africa, d) Southern Africa and e) Western Africa. The Rules of Procedure also provide for other types of caucuses to be established to deal with issues of common interest as the PAP deems necessary. There are two such caucuses: a) Women, b) Youth. Under rule 28, the caucuses meet in ordinary session twice a year during parliamentary sessions. Each caucus has a bureau comprising a chairperson, deputy chairperson and rapporteur.

The Pan-African Parliament Trust Fund was established on 26 May 2005 to promote: good governance; transparency and democracy; peace, security and stability; gender equality; and development in the integration of African people within Africa and other nations. The Fund is also expected to support the fight against HIV/AIDS, hunger and poverty in Africa.[49]

Electoral Contestation in Africa

Electoral contestation in Africa has unfolded in its larger security canvas, which has been shaped by a cumulative of factors. These include arbitrary territorial demarcation by the colonial powers ignoring the pre-existing ethno-tribal fabrics,[50] Cold War encampments of the super powers containing the functional interface between the political regimes and the citizenry, consequent restriction of the demographic cohesion in the post-colonial societies,[51] and increasingly selective unilateral post-Cold War interventions or threat of such interventions by the supra-state actors, assisted by the extra-regional powers, into the continent in the guise of 'international mandate.'

The insecurity in Africa is linked to competition between dominant global powers and new challengers over the continent's economic space, notably its resource base. The rising significance of emerging powers in Africa has resulted in more securitization of commercial stakes by external powers. The political dissent has selectively been used by some of these actors as strategic opportunities in the specific African countries. In some cases, this has resulted in disproportionate and irresponsible military interventions, creating scope for further security unrest in the continent. For instance, the North Atlantic Treaty Organization (NATO) forces had provided arms and related logistical support to the Islamist groups in their campaign against Gadafi in Libya in the year 2011.[52] In this respect, a United Nations (UN) report published in April 2013 stated, "Illicit flows from [Libya] are fuelling existing conflicts in Africa and the Levant and enriching the arsenals of a range of non-state actors, including terrorist groups."[53]

Above all, human security crisis is the top most concern in Africa. The continent's integration into world economy has unleashed unprecedented economic growth, bringing simultaneous problems concerning service distribution and opportunity access for its people. Under economic globalization process, the decade-long decline in poverty rate in much of Africa coincides with growing inequities at national and regional levels, and with respect to the rest of the world. Based on gender, rural/urban location and family income considerations, there is an increase in access disparity to basic services, such as food, water, health care, sanitation and education across the continent.

The cumulative complexity of the continent's security milieu is compounded by the partisan dereliction of the domestic ethno-political dispensation of the African countries, resulting in constant electoral contestation. The multi-party system in Africa has, indeed, been externally imposed through Structural Adjustment Programme of the Bretton Woods System. The competitive claims over electoral mandates have, many a time, led to ethno-political violent contestations. This has constrained the consolidation of procedural democracy in the politically 'aspirational and polarized' countries in Africa, weakening their integrating institutional mechanisms.

Electoral violence does pose a daunting paradox.[54] In theory, democratic electoral processes offer genuinely peaceful means to distribute political power within a society.[55] Indeed, in some Sub-Saharan Africa countries that transitioned from authoritarianism in the 1990s, electoral cycles have served to embed a more democratic system capable of peacefully regulating political competition. In other countries the electoral contest is associated with widespread violence. One of the common manifestations of electoral violence – seen in Kenya in 2007–2008 and Ivory Coast in 2000 – is opposition protest against electoral results, followed by violent government repression and generalized violence.[56]

The deeper aspect of violent electoral contestation is complexity of voting motivations which have significant bearing on the outcomes of multiparty elections in Africa. While ethnic sentiments play a role in shaping vote choice, it is noted that rational calculations about material welfare are apparently at the forefront of voters' minds. Thus a track record of social and economic delivery also counts for consistent re-election or power transition. As for ethno-electoral consideration, it is found that the principal line of ethnic cleavage in the context of electoral competition is whether individuals are 'insiders' or 'outsiders' to the prevailing distribution of political power. In other words, an individual's membership in the largest ethnic group and distrust of ethnic strangers play almost no role in shaping a vote for the political status quo. Instead, an individual's membership in the ethnic group that currently holds political power is a powerful factor explaining a vote for the ruling party. Conversely, an intention vote for the opposition is driven mainly by whether an individual feels a collective sense of ethnic discrimination.[57]

Nevertheless, instrumental expressions of partisanship do get prominent reflection in the voting behavior of the African electorates. Even as African voters increasingly seek to use voting rights to hold political leaders accountable for economic performance, they tend to encounter the institutional constraints of party and patronage systems inherited from a recent postcolonial past.[58]

To understand the causes of electoral violence, it is important to scrutinize the functioning of the institutions governing the electoral processes. Although contextual factors need to be considered, including the general role of elections as peaceful distributors of political power within a society and its previous history of conflict, the study suggests that inclusive electoral management bodies (EMBs) have played decisive roles in the reduction of electoral violence by preventing the opposition from taking to the streets and challenge the incumbent, which at times may create escalatory dynamics. Rather than solely aiming at producing conditions for granting the 'free and fair' label, the international community might be best advised to find ways to support collaborative and trust-building relationships between the EMBs and political parties to prevent conflict.[59]

AU's Moderating Role

The African Union (AU) has accorded a prominent position to democracy by recognizing its credibility as an enabling choice system that fosters economic growth and stability. Its growing commitment to democracy, being encapsulated by distinctly evolving African legal instruments, indicates the significant role that Africa plays in placing 'democratic entitlement' on international agenda. The AU through its several intergovernmental-cooperation mechanisms, indeed, tries to establish a firm link between the parallel process of integration and democratization in Africa, and it promotes the ideals and practice of political freedom within the world's second largest continent.[60]

The Constitutive Act of the AU has marked a new era in institution-building in post-colonial Africa. It is conceived as an aspect of Africa's response to the challenges of globalization and regional integration. The Constitutive Act, amended in January 2007 at Addis Ababa, Ethiopia, in principle is a catalyst for building a culture of peace and political stability in Africa. [61] The AU Charter on Democracy, Elections and Governance, adopted therein, has four main areas of focus: a) democracy, human rights and rule of law; b) elections and democratic institutions; c) unconstitutional changes of government; and d) political, economic and social governance. Its main objectives are to reinforce commitment to democracy, development and peace, based on principles similar to those expressed in the AU Constitutive

Act and the African Charter on Human and Peoples' Rights. Chapter 3 of the Democracy Charter contains the underlying principles as already recognized in the Constitutive Act of the AU:[62]

Article 3

State Parties shall implement this Charter in accordance with the following principles:

1. Respect for human rights and democratic principles;

2. Access to and exercise of state power in accordance with the constitution of the State Party and the principle of the rule of law;

3. Promotion of a system of government that is representative;

4. Holding of regular, transparent, free and fair elections;

5. Separation of powers;

6. Promotion of gender equality in public and private institutions;

7. Effective participation of citizens in democratic and development processes and in governance of public affairs;

8. Transparency and fairness in the management of public affairs;

9. Condemnation and rejection of acts of corruption, related offences and impunity;

10. Condemnation and total rejection of unconstitutional changes of government;

11. Strengthening political pluralism and recognising the role, rights and responsibility of legally constituted political parties, including opposition political parties, which should be given a status under national law.[63]

Chapter 5 contains provisions dealing with the development and maintenance of a 'culture of democracy and peace'. Article 11 provides that state parties must undertake to develop the necessary legislative and policy frameworks to establish and strengthen a culture of democracy and peace, and Article 12 mentions the necessity of implementing programmes and carrying out activities designed to promote democratic principles and practices as well as to consolidate a culture of democracy and peace. These programmes and activities should include promoting good governance; strengthening political institutions; creating conducive conditions for civil society organisations to exist and operate within the law; and integrating civic education into educational curricula. Article 13 of the charter states that 'State Parties shall take measures to ensure and maintain political and social dialogue, as well as public trust and transparency between political leaders and the people, in order to consolidate democracy and peace.'[64]

The African [Banjul] Charter on Human and Peoples' Rights, adopted on June 27, 1981 by the OAU, also provides in Article 13 (1) that '[e]very citizen shall have the right to participate freely in the government of his [sic] country ....'[65]

There has been exponential growth in elections in Africa, when most of its countries went for multi-party rule since the early 1990s. With the growth in elections has come the development and institutionalisation of election observation activities. In response to the democratic waves on the continent, the AU, a 54-member Pan-African organisation created in 2002 as a successor organisation to the OAU, has developed norms intended to promote political participation, improve electoral standards and facilitate the consolidation of democracy in member states. Thus the AU's Constitutive Act (2002), the OAU/AU Declaration on the Principles Governing Democratic Elections in Africa (2002), the Africa Charter on Democracy, Elections and Governance (2007), and the Guidelines for AU Electoral Observation and Monitoring Missions provide the benchmarks for the promotion of democratic elections.[66]

Steps towards ensuring that the AU played a leading role in enhancing electoral standards through election observation in Africa culminated in the creation of the Democracy and Electoral Assistance Unit (DEAU) in the Department of Political Affairs (DPA) of the African Union Commission (AUC) in 2008 to coordinate the election observation activities of the AU. The DEAU's mandates are to promote democracy and democratic elections within the continent by coordinating and organizing AU election observer missions to member states of the Union; and enhancing the national electoral processes of member states through the provision of direct technical and electoral assistance to election management bodies (EMBs) in Africa.[67]

Since DEAU's operation, election observation activities by the AU have become an important component of the *raison d'être* of the Organisation, and AU election observers have been deployed in almost all the 54 member states. The AU has published its Election Observation Manual in 2013, mentioning that currently the AU deploys on an average 15 Election Observation Missions on the continent annually. In 2011 alone, there were over 20 elections (presidential, parliamentary and referendums) in which the AU deployed observers.[68]

The mandate of the AU to observe elections in member states is based on the principle that "democratic elections are the basis of the authority of any government." Democratic elections should be conducted "freely and fairly" and "by impartial, all-inclusive competent accountable electoral institutions" in a manner of meeting international standards. Election observation by the AU, along with other international actors and domestic civil society organisations contributes to safeguarding electoral standards and thereby prevents post-election violence emanating from electoral disputes. The AU has, therefore, gradually over the years emerged as the dominant and leading guarantor of democratic elections and election observation in Africa.[69]

Election in Zimbabwe

The African Union observer mission in Zimbabwe has declared that the presidential elections were 'free, honest and credible.'[70] In response to the invitation by the Government of the Republic of Zimbabwe and the Zimbabwe Electoral Commission (ZEC) H.E Dr. Nkosazana Dlamini-Zuma, the Chairperson of the African Union Commission (AUC), deployed an African Union Election Observation Mission (AUEOM) to Zimbabwe to observe the Harmonized Elections held on 31July 2013. The AUEOM took place from 21 July to 6 August 2013 and was preceded by African Union (AU) Long Term Observers (LTOs) who arrived in Zimbabwe on 15 June and remained in the country until 14 August 2013.[71]

The AUEOM was led by H.E, Olusegun Obasanjo, former President of the Federal Republic of Nigeria as Head of Mission and H.E. Dr Aisha Abdullahi, African Union Commissioner for Political Affairs, as Deputy Head of Mission. The AUEOM comprised 69 observers (long term and short term) drawn from members of the Pan-African Parliament, members of the Permanent Representative Committee (PRC) of the African Union in Addis Ababa, Election Management Bodies (EMBs) and African Civil

Society Organisations from the following countries: Nigeria, Cameroon, Gabon, Mauritius, Ethiopia, Djibouti, Algeria, Saharawi Republic, Zambia, Namibia. Lesotho, Burkina Faso, Cote d'Ivoire, Libya, South Africa, Kenya, Tanzania, Gambia, South Sudan, Uganda, Sierra Leone and Botswana.[72]

The AUEOM was supported by a team of experts from the AUC, the Pan-African Parliament (PAP) and the Electoral Institute for Sustainable Democracy in Africa (EISA). H.E. Dr. Nkosazana Dlamini-Zuma, Chairperson of the AUC paid a working visit to the Republic of Zimbabwe from 24 to 26 July 2013.[73]

Regime Change in Libya

Libya witnessed a full-scale uprising in the early part of 2011 in protest against late Colonel Muammar Gaddafi, who had wrested the country's political power by carrying out a military coup since 1969. This revolt began in Benghazi of Eastern Libya, after popular movements crystallising under the Arab Spring overturned the rulers of Tunisia and Egypt in the North African neighbourhood. Gaddafi's regime tried to militarily suppress the opposition forces, which established the National Transitional Council (NTC) in Benghazi to administer the areas under their control. The NTC received France's immediate recognition as the 'legitimate government' of Libya.[74]

The UNSC responded to the crisis by adopting its Resolution 1970 warning Libyan authorities for their crimes against humanity and reminding the responsibility to protect their people.[75] With no positive difference to the crisis situation, the UNSC passed another Resolution 1973 sanctioning the establishment of a no-fly zone and the use of 'all means necessary' to protect civilians within Libya, with a 10–0 vote and five abstentions. While the resolution was supported by all the three African non-permanent members of the UNSC namely South Africa, Nigeria and Gabon, the abstentions included China and Russia with the veto power, as well as non-permanent members such as Brazil, Germany and India.[76]

Notwithstanding the abstaining member countries' concerns on the Resolution's implementation modality, limits to the military intervention, and avoiding human casualty and regional destabilisation, the North Atlantic Treaty Organisations (NATO) led by France went ahead with operations Odyssey Dawn and Ellamy. Amidst NATO's military intervention, the

African Union (AU) tried to mediate by proposing immediate and monitored cease-fire, and subsequent democratic elections. The AU's peace strategy was unconditionally accepted by the Gaddafi government. The NATO-backed NTC, however, refused to negotiate on its demand for Gaddafi's immediate abdication of power, leading to a protracted armed confrontation in Libya.[77]

The Arab League provided the sustained support for the military intervention in Libya due its leadership's antagonistic connection with Gaddafi, [78] who was championing the cause of Pan-Africanism and the AU's empowerment.[79] The NATO flaunted Arab League's consent as the justification to continue its regime-change exercise and deliberately undermined the AU's mediation initiative. Thus, the provision of involving regional organisations in the containment of conflict, as emphasised in both the 2001 ICISS Report and 2005 World Summit Outcome Document, was manipulated by the extra-regional powers while intervening in Libya.

The NTC finally captured capital Tripoli, with the subsequent gruesome killing of Gaddafi after allegedly being caught from his hometown Sirte on 20 October 2011.[80] While Libyan cities were falling into the NTC's fold, the secret detention of thousands of Gaddafi loyalists and the targeted attack on the Sub-Saharan Africans living in the country became a reality, evoking the United Nations High Commissioner for Refugees' call for the protection of rights and lives of the beleaguered community. Amnesty International in August 2011 estimated that between one third and half of those detained were from the Sub-Saharan Africa. Some African women alleged their rape by rebels in the refugee camps, with the reportage of forced labour. Foreign aid workers claimed to be prohibited from officially talking about the allegations.[81]

Still worse, post-Gaddafi Libya witnessed the eruption of intermittent clashes among tribal militias and the increase in violent crimes committed by uniformed men. The hundreds of heavily armed militias continue to indulge in clashes and defy orders from the NTC to disband or join the army and security forces.[82] While elections for a General National Congress were held in Libya in July 2012, the euphoria of success for holding the country's 'first free national election' in six decades was blighted with the killing of four American nationals including Ambassador Chris Stevens at the US consulate in Benghazi on 11 September 2012 amidst violent protest against the anti-Islam Innocence of Muslims video.[83] Thus, the actual political cost of intervention in Libya became clearer in the period of transition, as per the prognosis of an Africanist like Mahmood Mamdani, who had characterised the anti-Gaddafi coalition comprising secular middle class activists, royalists, tribalists and the radical Islamists.[84]

Beyond Libya, the change in Gaddafi regime has triggered ethno-political frictions spreading across the North Africa. Persecution of the alleged pro-Gaddafi Tuareg, a distinct nomadic community settling in several countries of the region, resulted in their flight from Libya to Mali where the political integration of their co-ethnic population was fragile under the colonial and post-colonial dispensations. Mali, in consequence, encountered with the intra-state battle, de facto territorial bifurcation, military coup and the increase in Islamist mobilisation. According to an UN estimate, more than 206,000 people were displaced in the country in the first half of 2012. While the Mali crisis has already elicited external intervention, Niger due to its sizable under-integrated Tuareg population remains the next theatre to fall into the regional chain of ethno-political destabilisation.[85]

The NATO's unilateral military intervention in Libya under the garb of R2P has, hence, caused enormous domestic and regional destabilisation. The brutal overthrow of the Gaddafi regime is, however, interpreted by an American Institutional Liberalist like Robert Keohane as one of the major indicators of the 'revival of moralism' in the post Cold-War world politics. Nevertheless, the purported moralpolitik motivations of the regime change in Libya are squarely exposed, when the US State Department raises its concerns for the sensitive oil contract documents lost during the attack on the American consulate in Benghazi. This reinforces Mahmood Mamdani's apprehension of more Libya like interventions in Africa, due to the contention between dominant global powers and new challengers over the continent's natural resources.[86]

What further strengthens the belief about offensive realpolitik objectives of the Western intervention in Libya is the startling revelation of a French secret agent killing Gaddafi by infiltrating the violent mob encircling him. The apparent purpose was to hush up the then French President Nicolas Sarkozy's suspicious links with the Libyan leader on the transfer of millions of dollar election campaign funds in 2007.[87] Libya's case, therefore, best explains the perception of the R2P as "ugly reality of geostrategic and commercial calculations camouflaged in the lofty rhetoric" in the Global South.[88]

After Gaddafi's ouster and death, a transitional government took charge and had the challenge of imposing order, disbanding the former rebel forces, rebuilding the economy, creating functioning institutions and managing the pledged transition to democracy and the rule of law. Elections for a General National Congress were held in July 2012, the country's first free national election in six decades. The congress appointed a prime minister, Ali Zeidan, in October, who formed an interim government tasked with preparing the ground for a new constitution and fresh parliamentary elections. However, tensions between nationalists and Islamists have stymied attempts to produce a stable government, and in 2014 the country was riven by fighting between rival militias. Central government collapsed, and the United Nations has struggled to bring political factions together.[89]

Endnotes

1   Daniel C. Bach (2011), "Patrimonialism and Neopatrimonialism: Comparative Trajectories and Readings," *Commonwealth & Comparative Politics*, 49 (3), p. 275

2   Daniel C. Bach and Mamoudou Gazibo, (Eds),   *Neopatrimonialism in Africa and Beyond*, New York: Routledge, 2011

3   J.-F. Me ́dard, (1979) L'E ́tat sous-de ́veloppe ́ au Cameroun, in: CEAN, *Anne ́e africaine 1977*, Paris: Pe ́done, p. 39.

4   Ibid, 1979, p. 68

5   D. Bourmaud, (1997) *La Politique en Afrique*, Paris: Montchrestien, p. 61

6   Bratton, M. & van de Walle, N. (1994), "Neopatrimonial Regimes and Political Transitions in Africa," *World Politics*, 46(4), p. 458.

7   Bourmaud, 1997, p. 62

8   van de Walle, N. (1994) Neopatrimonialism and Democracy in Africa, with an illus- tration from Cameroon, in: J. Widner (Ed.) *Economic Change and Political Liberalization in Sub-Saharan Africa*, Baltimore: Johns Hopkins University Press, p. 131.

9   Me ́dard, J.-F. (2000) L'E ́tat et le politique en Afrique, *Revue franc ̧aise de science poli- tique*, 50(4),p. 854.

10 J.-P. Olivier de Sardan, (1999) A Moral Economy of Corruption in Africa? *Journal of Modern African Studies*, 37(1), pp. 25–52.

11 Bourmaud, D. (1991) L'E 'tat centrifuge au Kenya, in: J.-F. Me 'dard (Ed.) *E 'tats d'Afrique noire: formations, me 'canismes et crise*, Paris: Karthala, p. 262.

12 J.-F. Me 'dard, (1987) Charles Njonjo: portrait d'un 'big man' au Kenya, in: E. Terray (Ed.) *L'E 'tat contemporain en Afrique*, Paris: l'Harmattan, pp. 49–87; Y.-A. Faure '& J.-F. Me 'dard (1995) L'E 'tat-business et les politiciens entrepreneurs. Ne 'o-patrimonialisme et Big Men:e 'conomie et politique, in: S. Ellis & Y.-A. Faure ' (Eds) *Entreprises et entrepreneurs africains*, pp. 289–309 (Paris: Karthala). Faure' & Me'dard, pp. 289–309.

13 R. C. Crook, "Patrimonialism, Administrative Effectiveness and Economic Development in Co ^te d'Ivoire," *African Affairs*, 88(351), 1989, p. 214

14 R. Sandbrook, (1985) *The Politics of Africa's Economic Stagnation*, Cambridge: Cambridge University Press, pp.119–121.

15 Crook, 1989, pp. 227–228

16 R. Theobald, (1982) "Patrimonialism," *World Politics*, 34(4), p. 550

17 J.-F. Me 'dard, (1991) L'E 'tat ne 'o-patrimonial en Afrique noire, J.-F. Me 'dard (Ed.) *E 'tats d'Afrique noire: formation, me 'canismes et crises*, Paris: Karthala, p. 339.

18 P. Englebert, (2000) *State Legitimacy and Development in Africa,* Boulder: Lynne Rienner, pp.104–105.

19 D. Bigo, (1988) *Pouvoir et obe 'issance en Centrafrique,* Paris: Karthala.

20 R. Lemarchand, (2003) The democratic republic of the Congo: from failure to potential reconstruction, in: R. I. Rotberg (Ed.) *State Failure and State Weakness in a Time of Terror,* Washington, DC: Brookings Institution Press, p. 31.

21 C. Young & T. Turner, (1985) *The Rise and Decline of the Zairian State,* Madison: University of Wisconsin Press, p.165.

22 H. E. Chehabi& J. J. Linz, (Eds) (1998) *SultanisticRegimes*, Baltimore: JohnsHopkins University Press.

23 M. Gazibo, (2006) *Introduction a ` la politique africaine*, Montre 'al: Presses de l'Universite ' de Montre 'al, p. 97.

24 P. M. Lewis, (1996) "From prebendalism to predation: the political economy of decline in Nigeria," *The Journal of Modern African Studies*, 34(1), pp. 79–103.

25 Daniel C. Bach, 2011.

26 This distinction borrows from Christian Geffray's discussion (2000: 15–20) of state and criminality in Brazil.

27 Timothy Murithi, "Briefing the African Union at Ten: An Appraisal," African Affairs, 111(445), 2012, p.668.

28 United Nations Conference on Trade and Development (UNCTAD), 'Trade performance and commodity dependence' (UNCTAD, Geneva, 26 February 2004).

29 Godwin Dogbey, 'Towards a strategic vision for a continent in distress' in Olubenga Adesida and Arunma Oteh (eds.), *African Voices, African Visions* (Nordic Africa Institute, Stockholm, 2001).

30 New Partnership for Africa's Development, 'The African Peer Review Mechanism' (Base Document, Sixth Summit of the NEPAD Heads of State and Government Implementation Committee, NEPAD/HSGIC/03-2003/APRM/MOU/Annex II, 9 March 2003, Abuja, Nigeria).

31 Ayesha Kajee, 'NEPAD's APRM: a progress report, practical limitations and challenges' in South African Yearbook of International Affairs (South African Institute of International Affairs, Johannesburg, 2004).

32 George Monbiot, 'At the seat of empire: Africa is forced to take the blame for the devastation inflicted on it by the rich world', The Guardian, 25 June 2002 <http://www.guardian. co.uk/politics/2002/jun/25/foreignpolicy.greenpolitics? INTCMP=SRCH> (1 July 2012)

33 This is based on findings of the author's field study in Addis Ababa, AU Headquarters, in December 2014.

34 "The African Governance Architecture and Its Platform," A Presentation by the Department of Political Affairs, www.au.int/en/sites/.../The%20African%20 Governace%20Platform.pptx

35 Ibid.

36 Ibid.

37 Ibid.

38   Ibid.

39   Ibid.

40   African Union Hand Book 2015, http://www.au.int/en/sites/default/files/MFA-AU-Handbook-2014-ENGLISH-v17%20interactive%281%29_0.pdf, p.82.

41   Ibid.

42   Ibid.

43   Ibid, p. 83.

44   Ibid.

45   Ibid.

46   Ibid, p. 84.

47   Ibid, p. 85.

48   Ibid, p. 86.

49   Ibid.

50   Mohammed Ayoob, "Inequalities and Theorizing in International Relations: The Case for Subaltern Realism", *International Studies Review*, 4(3), Autumn 2002, pp.37-46.

51   Robert H. Jackson (1993), *Quasi-States: Sovereignty, International Relations and the Third World*, Cambridge: Cambridge University Press, p.23.

52   Sandipani Dash, " Responsibility to Protect: The Case of Libya", 04 December 2012, http://www.icwa.in/pdfs/IBresponsibilitytoprotect.pdf

53   Noureddine Jebnoun, "Changing Security Dynamics in North Africa and Western Sahel Region", *Portuguese Journal of International Affairs*, Spring/Summer 2014, p.9.

54   Christian Opitz, Hanne Fjelde & Kristine Höglund (2013), "Including Peace: The Influence of Electoral Management Bodies on Electoral Violence", *Journal of Eastern African Studies*, 7(4), p. 713.

55   Robert Alan Dahl (1973), *Polyarch: Participation and Opposition*, New Haven: Yale University Press.

56   Christian Opitz, op.cit.

57 Michael Bratton, Ravi Bhavnani & Tse-Hsin Chen (2012), "Voting intentions in Africa: Ethnic, Economic or Partisan?," *Commonwealth & Comparative Politics*, 50 (1), pp. 46-47.

58 Ibid., p.48.

59 Christian Opitz, op.cit., pp.726-7.

60 Michele Olivier, "The Emergence of a Right to Democracy-An African Perspective", in Carlo Panara and Gary Wilson (Ed.), *The Arab Spring: New Patterns for Democracy and International Law*, 2013, Leiden and Boston: Martinus Nijhoff, pp. 29-52.

61 AISA Policy Brief, "Unconstitutional Changes of Government in Africa: An Assessment of the Relevance of the Constitutive Act of the African Union", No. 44, March 2011 http://www.ai.org.za/wp-content/uploads/downloads/2011/11/No-44.-Unconstitutional-Changes-of-Government-in-Africa.pdf

62 Narnia Bohler-Muller, "Is Democracy a 'Shared Value' that Unites Africa?" *AISA Policy Brief*, No. 59, September 2011, http://www.ai.org.za/wp-content/uploads/downloads/2011/11/No-59.-Is-Democracy-a-Shared-vallue-that-Unites-Africa.pdf

63 Ibid.

64 Ibid.

65 Ibid.

66 AU, Election Observation Manual, 2013, http://www.au-elections.org/documents/auob.pdf

67 Ibid; Also see AU, Elections, http://www.au-elections.org/

68 Ibid.

69 Ibid.

70 BBC News, Zimbabwe election 'free and fair', say AU observers, 2 August 2013 http://www.bbc.com/news/world-africa-23550191

71 African Union Election Observation Mission Report: Zimbabwe, 2013, http://pa.au.int/en/sites/default/files/AUEOM%20REPORT%20ZIMBABWE%202013.pdf

72 Ibid.

73   Ibid.

74   "Libya: France recognises rebels as government", *BBC News*, 10 March 2011, http://www.bbc.co.uk/news/world-africa-12699183, Accessed on 14 August 2011

75   United Nations, S/RES/1970, "Peace and Security in Africa", 2011, http://www.un.org/ga/search/view_doc.asp?symbol=S/RES/1970(2011) , Accessed on 15 September 2011

76   United Nations, S/RES/1973, 2011, "Libya", http://www.un.org/ga/search/view_doc.asp?symbol=S/RES/1973(2011), Accessed on 15 September 2012; Yash Tandon, "Whose Dictator is Qaddafi? The Empire and its Neo-Colonies", *Insight on Africa*, 3 (1), 2011, pp.1-21

77   "Libya: Benghazi rebels reject African Union truce plan", *BBC News*, 11 April 2011, http://www.bbc.co.uk/news/world-africa-13035501, Accessed on 16 June 2011

78   Michael Slackman, "Dislike for Qaddafi Gives Arabs a Point of Unity", *New York Times*, 21 March 2011, http://www.nytimes.com/2011/03/22/world/africa/22arab.html, Accessed on 20 September 2012

79   Ademola Abass, "African Peace and Security Architecture and the Protection of Human Security", in Ademola Abass (Ed.), *Protecting Human Security in Africa,* New York: Oxford University Press, 2010, pp.261-262

80   Ibid.

81   Amnesty International, "Detention Abuses Staining The New Libya", October 2011, www.amnesty.org/sites/impact.amnesty.org/.../mde190362011en.pdf, Accessed on 11 December 2011

82   Donatella Rovera, "Time to Crack Down on Libya's New Torturers, *World Today*, April 2012, http://www.chathamhouse.org/sites/default/files/public/The%20World%20Today/2012/april/0412rovera.pdf, Accessed on 14 September 2012

83   "Libya Profile", *BBC News*, 12 September 2012, http://www.bbc.com/news/world-africa-13754897, Accessed on 18 September 2012; Suhasini Haidar, "Facing an Inconvenient Truth", *The Hindu,* 26 September 2012, http://www.thehindu.com/opinion/op-ed/facing-an-inconvenient-truth/article3935884.ece, Accessed on 27 September 2012

84   Mahmood Mamdani, "Libya: Politics of Humanitarian Intervention" 31   Mar   2011,   *Al   Jazeera*,   http://www.aljazeera.com/indepth/

opinion/2011/03/201133111277476962.html, Accessed on 15 September 2012

85 "U.S. denounces film's content", *The Hindu*,15 September 2012, http://www.thehindu.com/todays-paper/tp-international/article3899266.ece, Accessed on 16 September 2012

86 Mahmood Mamdani, "What does Gaddafi's fall mean for Africa?", *Al Jazeera*, 26 October 2011, http://www.aljazeera.com/indepth/opinion/2011/08/201182812377546414.html, Accessed on 15 September 2012

87 "French agent shot Gaddafi on Sarkozy's orders", *Indian Express*, 02 October 2012, http://www.indianexpress.com/news/-french-agent-shot-gaddafi-on-sarkozy-s-orders-/1010552/2, Accessed on 03 October 2012

88 Ramesh Thakur, one of the 12 authors of ICISS Report, quoted in W. Andy Knight & Frazer Egerton (Ed.) (2012), *The Routledge Handbook on The Responsibility to Protect*, Oxon: Routledge p.259

89 BBC News, Libya Country Profile – Overview, http://www.bbc.com/news/world-africa-13754897

Chapter – 4

Economic Security in Africa: AU's Response

Africa is rapidly shedding the stigma of a marginal and 'dispensable' region.[1] Beyond the lure of commodities and natural resources, investors and businessmen emphasize the attractiveness of sustained growth rates, and the strong potential for market expansion generated by urbanisation and the empowerment of new socio-economic categories. The depictions of Africa as an attractive new 'frontier' and 'emerging' continent[2] are rooted in the postulate that the continent is on the verge of a wave of region-building that will overcome the current fragmentation of markets.[3] Region-building in Africa still remains heavily constrained by the complex institutional blueprints formally adopted by regional organisations that pretend to emulate the experience of the European Union (EU). It is also necessary to address as to what 'new' regionalism has come to stand for. It will be argued that the value of this notion is unquestionable from an analytical standpoint, despite the disappointing achievements of the regional organisations that have sought to surf on the wave of new regionalism. The revival of regionalism has, in Africa, been en-tête de page paire paradoxically associated with the endorsement of institutional blueprints drawn from the European experience. The outcome has been the development of 'thick' institutionalism as the ambitious institutionalisation processes prescribed are yet to be matched by prescribed transfers of sovereignty or the implementation of common policies. The implications of such a dysfunctional process can no longer be overlooked at a time when European integration is, within Europe itself, facing a severe crisis. The article concludes with a brief discussion of the implications of radical shifts in Africa's interactions with the global economy and how they may stimulate a 'look east' approach to the defragmentation of African markets and policies.[4]

This chapter has assessed AU's response to economic resurgence in Africa in terms of providing order and stability as prerequisite of economic take off. It will look at post-secession conflict between Sudan and South concerning their conjoined oil industry and AU's meditational role in bringing the two parties to the negotiating table for working solution to the problems.

Economic Integration and its Politics

In post-colonial Africa, the trajectories of regional organizations relate to a distinctive history, shaped by the legacy of three waves of institution-building. The first wave was a spill-over effect of the dissolution of the federations and common services established under colonial rule. As most African federations were being dismantled on the eve of independence, their common services often survived, generally as IGOs meant to manage common assets.[5] In two cases only, the Southern African Customs Union (SACU) and the CFA Franc currency zone, the transformation of colonial arrangement into hegemonic regimes would result in unique instances of integration through "hysteresis".[6]

The rise of the second generation of regional organizations was largely driven by geopolitical considerations, including when economic cooperation or integration were the stated objectives. Most of the groupings meant to promote regional economic integration combined aspirations to import-substitution industrialization (ISA) with strong inspiration from the (then) European Economic Community's constitutional approach to integration. Throughout the period of the Cold War, the politics of competing affiliations and patronage ties prevailed over the implementation of commonly stated economic goals. The politics of "bloc building" still represent a key aspect of present day regional politics in Africa, as the intractable problems of multiple membership (the so-called rationalization debates) show.[7]

Most of the regional integration organizations established in the 1970s and 1980s are still functioning, but their mandates, institutional architecture and acronyms went through drastic overhauls in the early 1990s. Unlike what was the case in other world regions, the revival of regionalism took an asymptomatic course in so far as, in Africa, the adoption of neo-liberal agendas went along with the endorsement of ambitious projects towards a constitutionalization of integration and the mutualization of sovereignties. The treaties of all the existing regional integration groupings were profoundly revised in the early 1990s and new acronyms were adopted to signal changing priorities: the Preferential Trade Area (PTA) of East and Southern Africa became the Common Market for East and Southern Africa (COMESA); in West Africa, the Communauté Economique de l'Afrique de l'Ouest (CEAO) was superseded by the West African Economic and Monetary Union (UEMOA); in central Africa, the Union Douanière et Economique de l'Afrique Centrale (UDEAC) was replaced by the Economic and Monetary Union of Central Africa (CEMAC), while in Southern Africa, the Southern African Development Coordination Conference (SADCC) morphed into a Southern African Development Community (SADC).

These transformations went along with pledges towards the adoption of transfers of sovereignty and the enforcement of good governance and rule of law agendas. By the end of the 1990s, protocols establishing security management architectures had also been adopted by two key regional organizations (ECOWAS and SADC). The revival of regionalism in the 1990s was also stimulated by the adoption of the Abuja Plan of Action. This continental blueprint prescribes the establishment of regional economic communities (RECs) that are to operate as building blocks towards an integrated African Economic Community (AEC) by 2028. By then, the AEC should involve the free movement of people and factors of production, a single domestic market, an economic and monetary union (with a single African currency) and a central bank. Today, eight regional groupings are officially recognized by the AU as RECs– the Arab Maghreb Union (AMU); the ECOWAS, COMESA, SADC, the Intergovernmental Authority for Development (IGAD), the Community of Sahel- Saharan States (CENSAD), the Economic Community of Central African States (ECCAS), and the East African Community (EAC).

The RECs and the African Union (AU), launched in 2002 following the revision of the OAU Charter, endorsed an approach to region-building that may be retrospectively described as a case of "thick" regionalism. Emphasis on institution-building and good governance within memberstates is expected to contribute to the progressive transformation of the AU and the RECs into effective agencies of restraint. The new Constitutive Act (CA) has considerably broadened the missions of the AU, since it now incorporates the establishment of the AEC and the creation of a sophisticated African Peace and Security Architecture (APSA) (Engel and Porto, this volume). APSA's ambitious agenda is rooted in the assertion of a normative revolution: the substitution of a culture of "non-indifference" to the pre-existing emphasis on strict "non-interference" in the internal affairs of member-states.[8]

As a result, the AU is the regional organization which, by world standards, carries the boldest provisions allowing intervention into the affairs of its member states. In accordance with these objectives, the transformation of the former Bureau of the OAU into a Peace and Security Council (PSC) aims at improving the conflict resolution and peace building capacity of the AU. The CA of the AU also provides for the creation of an Economic, Social and Cultural Council (ECOSOCC), for the establishment of an African Court on Human and Peoples' Rights (ACHPR), and for a Pan-African parliament.

The establishment of Free Trade Areas (FTAs) and customs unions within the RECs was originally meant to have taken place within, respectively, ten and twelve years following the adoption of the Abuja treaty in 1991. Two decades later, AMU, CENSAD and IGAD are nowhere near establishing FTAs. In the Maghreb, member-states of the AMU have not been able to meet for several years. In the Horn of Africa, IGAD is still primarily a political forum, while CENSAD is probably doomed to fade into oblivion with the eviction of its Libyan patron and financier, Muammar Gadhafi. While ECOWAS, ECCAS and the EAC have formally announced the establishment of their FTAs, SADC is yet to achieve this objective despite the formal claim (on its website) that the FTA was launched in 2008.

Current assessments of the state of regional economic integration in Africa, while celebrating the region's transformation into a "new frontier" for international trade and investment, also observe that region-building is severely hampered by what amounts to a collection of fragmented small economies.[9] The regionalization of markets and policies still remains embryonic. There is a striking contrast between the dynamism of the so-called "informal" trade and the quasi-irrelevance (11 per cent) of recorded intraregional flows, compared to what is observed in Europe (72 per cent) and Asia (52 per cent).[10]

This reflects on the poor implementation of stated agendas, but also on the intrinsic limitations of approaches to regional integration that, as in Europe, should require significant transfers of sovereignty. Whereas the construction of Europe is dotted with a succession of hard-fought compromises that have resulted in the deepening of its institutionalization and a constitutionalization process, the RECs emphasis on institution-building and endorsement of the EU model has remained purely formal. The outcome is an ad hoc situation best described as a case of "thick" institutionalism due to a total disconnect between pledges and effective implementation, unlike the EU's effective institutionalization processes or ASEAN's explicitly assumed "lean" institutional blueprints.[11]

Neopatrimonial State and Regionalization in Africa

The EAC is the only African regional economic grouping that has officially graduated from a FTA into a customs union. Eight years after the initial adoption of the Customs Union Protocol, concrete steps towards implementation were still being awaited.[12] The track record the EAC, one of the most successful regional groupings in Africa, is a reminder that the ability of regional organizations to implement intrusive institutional agendas presumes that member-states concede to a reduction of national prerogatives and territorial control. Agreement to transfer and "pool" sovereignties in specific areas postulates a capacity and willingness to do so, an issue that refers in fine to the production and implementation of public policies that do not simply reflect upon the private interests of the ruler and his clients. As the following chapters in this section make clear, Africa's regional and sub-regional organizations were, until the reversal of the (O)AU agenda in the early 2000s, exclusively focused on protecting and consolidating established regimes and interests.

The limited capacity of African regional organizations to implement their ambitious economic agendas cannot be simply attributed to the existence or absence of supranational decision-making or to a lack of political will on the part of member-states. Thick institutionalism enhances the adverse effects of the coexistence, within African regional and continental groupings, of thoroughly patrimonialized and predatory regimes, along with states within which neopatrimonialism is capped, regulated or ring-fenced. Procrastination over the dismantlement of tariff and non-tariff barriers may result from openly acknowledged policy orientations. It is an altogether issue when a state falls short of implementing decisions that are legally binding.[13]

Neopatrimonialism also nurtures and stimulates specific patterns of regionalization, in conjunction with the exploitation of cross-border opportunities. The blanket term of informal trade invites a focus on cross-border transactions that follow traditional routes and reflect upon natural complementarities. These transactions are often of great significance to the populations living in the borderlands. What we have labelled "transstate regionalization" refers to the ability of transnational players to transact across territories and borders, thanks to complicities within state institutions. The dynamism of trans-state networks proceeds from the ability to avoid or negotiate border enforcement policies, often through complicities within state bureaucracies.[14]

The reach of trans-state networks goes well beyond the borderland, although it is there that their activity gains greater visibility. Their dynamism builds upon the instrumentalization of opportunities generated by tariff, fiscal, monetary or normative discrepancies. Transactions can involve the transit of commodities (exploitation of disparities between producer prices on each side of the border), but also long-distance trade in products like alcohol, cigarettes or petroleum, or the circulation of more sophisticated items such as cell phones, computer equipment, vehicles, medicine, diamonds, endangered species, drugs, and of course arms. Trans-state networks capitalize on the permeation of public policies by private interest. Variable geometry in interpreting national regulations is central to the profitability of such transactions, as Mahaman Tijani Alou's detailed analysis of the customs services in Niger illustrates.[15]

Trans-state networks cut across borders-lines and penetrate state institutions, but they do not seek to challenge the territorial status quo: it is the preservation of strong disparities across the border that stimulates what is presented, depending on circumstances, as smuggling, informal, unofficial, illicit or re-export trade. One of the outcomes is the emergence of spaces that are largely autonomous from the territorially defined regions that the RECs are meant to build. Indeed, trans-state networks, like informal trade in general, revolve around social, religious or geo-ethnic affiliations as opposed to territorially-based identities.

Trans-state interactions can, in some cases, relate to institutionally-driven policy orientations. Throughout the 1980s and 1990s, the opportunities associated with transit-trade were carefully nurtured by the entrepot states of coastal West Africa where policy-makers adopted enabling legal and fiscal frameworks. At the other end of the spectrum, the dissolution of some states into informality, as in the Horn of Africa, has contributed to draw the contours of a radically different regional landscape. The pre-eminence of networks over policies is stimulated by the rich opportunities associated with the dividends of the frontier, not to mention those drawn from the "dividends" of violence and insecurity.[16]

Regional conflicts generate their own brand of regionalization whenever the spread of violence and insecurity contributes to nurture an alternative system of access to profit, power and protection. Like the above mentioned-case of Somalia, the conflicts in and around the DRC also offer a near perfect example of the decisive influence of "transboundary networks, some illicit some not".[17]

(De)fragmentation of African Markets

As the Eurozone sovereign debt crisis gained a new acuity in early 2012, Africa ranked second after Asia among the regions identified by international investors as dynamic and least affected by the effects of the global financial crisis.[18] Beyond the lure of commodities and natural resources, investors and businessmen emphasize the attractiveness of sustained growth rates, and the strong potential for market expansion generated by urbanization and the empowerment of new socio-economic categories. Investment flows into the continent have surpassed aid flows since 2006, and private investors have a clear focus on markets that have a regional potential as hubs. The outcome is fresh incentives to pragmatism that fuel defragmentation in the field of banking and finance (viz the success of the Ecobank in West Africa), through the adoption of measures designed to reduce of the cost of doing business (Common Investment Area within COMESA), the rehabilitation of infrastructures, and the establishment of corridors of growth combining public with private support (as successfully initiated by the Maputo Development Corridor over a decade ago).[19]

More generally, Africa's improving terms of engagement within the global economy generate their own "structural" pressure towards the defragmentation of markets beyond national boundary-lines and the regional economic groupings within which they are meant to dissolve. So as to anticipate the intractable problems generated by the combination of multiple affiliations to RECs that might result in mutually incompatible Common External Tariff (CET) agreements, a newly established arena, the African trade forum, is now discussing the creation of a continental FTA. In Southern and Eastern Africa, South African ambitions to fulfil the country's potential as a regional hub and a gateway to the continent, underscore the country's support for the establishment of a tripartite (COMESA-EAC-SADC) FTA, [20] which has taken a concrete shape.

Similarly, the AU has launched a pan-African passport. The idea behind the initiative is that the free movement of people would help create jobs and stimulate economic activity. This, in turn, would increase intra-African trade, boosting economic growth. The organisation's intention is that by 2018 the passport would be distributed to all African citizens. The AU envisages the issuing of a biometric passport, or electronic passport, which would use contactless smart-card technology. It was chosen instead of a traditional passport because there is a smaller chance of fraud. The concept has been strongly backed by a number countries, such as the Seychelles, Mauritius, Senegal and Rwanda. All have eased or lifted visa requirements for people travelling from other African countries. While the idea of adopting a unique e-passport for Africans is certainly exemplary, there are apprehension of social, cultural and, above all, economic issues that might make the use of this passport impractical.[21]

Conceptualising New Regionalism

New regionalism stands first and foremost for new patterns of expression and understanding of issues that used to be more narrowly conceived through the notion of integration.[22] In accordance with a now well-established thread of analysis, regionalism refers in this paper to cognitive or state-centric projects, while regionalisation points to processes and de facto outcomes. Regionalism refers to ideas or ideologies, programs, policies and goals that seek to transform an identified social space into a regional project. Since regionalism postulates the implementation of a program and the definition of a strategy, it is often associated with institution-building or the conclusion of formal agreements. Regionalism can also relate to the production, invention or re-invention of transnational identities, a process concomitant with the delineation of mental maps and boundaries.[23]

By contrast, regionalisation focuses on the build up of interactions which may or may not relate to an explicitly asserted or acknowledged regionalist project. Regionalisation is a more encompassing notion than regionalism since it takes into account processes and configurations within which states are frequently not the key players. Regionalisation may correlate with the implementation of regionalist strategies and translate into processes of cross-border integration. Regionalism may equally, as mentioned above, involve a loss of state territorial control and the emergence of autonomous regional spaces. Regionalisation can grow irrespective of state policies, and even at times, in opposition to their stated purpose. In West Africa as in Asia, trade or migration networks do not have the ambition to build regional integration per se. Regionalization, as it is being promoted by the Yoruba or Hausa trade diasporas in West Africa, proceeds from the aggregation of the strategies of micro-economic agents. Regionalisation can also be the outcome of corporate strategies by firms, ranging from small business ventures to the large multinationals, seeking to enhance their competitive edge.

Regionalism is more axiologically neutral than the concept of regional integration for it involves a broader understanding of what region-building and regionness may be about.[24] The notion of regionalism offers a long overdue insight into the paradox whereby, as Axline already lamented in the 1970s, "most cases of regional integration are among Third World countries, yet research in this field has been dominated by theory based on the European experience".[25] Regionalism accommodates an extreme heterogeneity of configurations, ranging from those involving the material organisation of transfers of sovereignty (regional integration) to cognitive and ideational projects (associated with the 'invention' of regions and construction of identities within existing states). Regionalism can account for integration processes, but can equally serve to monitor disintegration, namely demands that challenge state sovereignty and border-lines. Unlike the notion of regional integration, regionalism has no difficulty to account for agendas which, as the track-record of ASEAN illustrates, seek to promote region-building through sovereignty 'enhancement' as opposed to sovereignty "pooling".[26]

Regionalism also enables the analyst to keep away from an underlying assumption associated with the concept of regional integration: the confusion generated by its undifferentiated association with goals and processes.[27] By contrast, the dichotomy between regionalism and regionalisation enables the analyst to account for configurations where, as frequently the case in Africa, regionalism and regionalization contribute to shape distinct regional landscapes.

The notions of regionalism and regionalisation free the analyst from the teleological and normative implications associated with 'integration'. Regionalism also offers a counterpoint to the treatment of Europe as the prototype for region-building since the 1950s. Empirically, 'new' regionalism stands for a wave of region-building that gathered stamina from the late 1980s onwards as neo-liberal policies unleashed the expansion of cross border networks and transnational interactions powered by non-state players.[28]

New Regionalism in Africa

European construction may be described as the outcome of a process of convergence between regionalism and regionalisation. A good illustration of its trajectory is the correlation between the EU's successive rounds of enlargement and the build-up of trade and investment interdependencies between old and new members -- the so called 'magnetic pull' of the EU over its neighbourhood. Such a postulate cannot be taken for granted in the case of Africa where regionalisation frequently thrives at the expense of state-centric regional agendas.

The revival of regionalism in the late 1980s was a global and largely unanticipated phenomenon. The de facto crystallization of trade and investment flows around the three core regions of the 'triad' owed much to the dynamism of non-state players. And when states were a driving force, this went along with significant policy-shifts in the mandates and agendas of established regional inter-governmental organizations (Landau, 1999; Fawcett: 1995). While implementation of the EU's Single European Market agenda (1986-1992) went on, in North America negotiations towards NAFTA (1991-1994) were proceeding. Since this momentum went along with the establishment of the WTO (1994) it stimulated debates on the functions of regionalism as 'master or servant' of multilateralism.[29] In Latin America and in Asia, it was the notion of "open regionalism" that would provide the backbone for rejuvenated agendas and the emergence of such new organisations as Mercosur. This ongoing wave of regionalism, branded as 'new regionalism', was generally associated with the promotion of less state- and euro-centric patterns of region-building. This has not been the case in Africa until very recently.

In post-colonial Africa, the discussion of regional integration relates to a distinctive history, shaped by the legacy of three threads of institution-building since colonial rule. The first generation was a spillover effect of the dissolution of the federations and common services established during the colonial period. As most of Africa's federations were being dismantled on the eve of independence, their common services often survived, generally as IGOs meant to manage common assets. In two cases, the Southern African Customs Union (SACU) and the CFA Franc currency zone, the transformation of colonial arrangement into hegemonic regimes resulted in unique instances of integration through hysteresis.[30]

The second generation of institution- building also emerged during the 1960s and was largely driven by geo-political considerations, including when economic cooperation or integration were the stated objectives. Most of the groupings meant to promote regional economic integration combined aspirations to import-substitution with strong inspiration from the (then) European Economic Community's 'constitutional' approach to integration. Throughout the period of the cold war, the politics of competing affiliations and patronage ties prevailed over the implementation of commonly stated economic goals. Most of the IGOs established during this period are still functioning, but their mandates, institutional architecture and acronyms went through drastic revisions in the early 1990s.

In Africa, the revival of regionalism took an asymptomatic course in so far as it retrospectively appears to have meant the endorsement of ambitious projects towards a constitutionalisation of integration and the mutualisation of sovereignties. The treaties of all the existing regional integration groupings were profoundly revised in the early 1990s and new acronyms were adopted to signal changing priorities: the Preferential Trade Area (PTA) of East and Southern Africa became the Common Market for East and Southern Africa (COMESA); in West Africa, the Communauté Economique de l'Afrique de l'Ouest (CEAO) was superseded by the West African Economic and Monetary Union (UEMOA); in central Africa, the Union Douanière et Economique de l'Afrique Centrale (UDEAC) was replaced by the Economic and Monetary Union of Central Africa (CEMAC), while in Southern Africa, the Southern African Development Coordination Conference (SADCC) morphed into a Southern African Development Community (SADC). These transformations went along with pledges towards the adoptions of transfers of sovereignty and the enforcement of good governance and rule of law agendas. By the end of the 1990s, protocols establishing security management architectures had also been adopted by two key regional organisations (ECOWAS and SADC).

These agendas were also designed so as to contribute to the implementation of the Abuja Plan of Action. Adopted in 1991, this continental blueprint prescribes the establishment of regional economic communities (RECs) that are to operate as 'building-blocks' towards an integrated African Economic Community (AEC) by 2028. By then, the AEC should involve the free movement of people and factors of production, a single domestic market, an economic and monetary union (with a single African currency) and a central bank. Today, eight regional groupings are officially recognized by the

AU as RECs – the Arab Maghreb Union (AMU); the ECOWAS, COMESA, SADC, the Intergovernmental Authority for Development (IGAD), the Community of Sahel-Saharan States (CENSAD), the Economic Community of Central African States (ECCAS), and the East African Community (EAC).

The African Union (AU), launched in 2002 following the revision of the OAU Charter, similarly reflects upon the endorsement of thick institutionalism as an overall approach to region-building. Emphasis on institution-building and good governance with member-states is expected to contribute to the progressive transformation of the AU and the RECs into effective 'agencies of restraint'.[31] The new Constitutive Act (CA) considerably broadens the missions of the AU since they now incorporate the establishment of the AEC and the creation of a sophisticated African Peace and Security Architecture (APSA). The APSA's establishment builds upon a normative revolution: the substitution of a culture of 'non-indifference' for the past principle of strict non interference in the internal affairs of member-states.[32] As a result, the AU became the regional organisation which, by world standards, carries the boldest provisions allowing intervention into the affairs of its member-states. In accordance with these objectives, the transformation of the former Bureau of the OAU into a Peace and Security Council (PSC) aims at improving the conflict resolution and peace-building capacity of the AU. The CA of the AU also provides for the creation of an Economic, Social and Cultural Council (ECOSOCC), for the establishment of an African Court on Human and Peoples' Rights (ACHPR), and for a Pan-African parliament.

The thick institutional agendas assigned to the RECs and the AU since the 1990s converge towards the construction of a continental economic and monetary union along with the mutualisation of sovereignties. All are strongly evocative of the trajectory followed by the EU. As the EAC and ECOWAS treaties illustrate, elements of federalism that go well beyond the EU's stated ambitions have been formally endorsed by some of the RECs.

More than in any other world region, the EEC/EU and its member-states have contributed to shape representations of regionalism and region-building in Africa. References to the EU as a prototype for region-building may be viewed as a tribute to the exemplary achievements of the European experience since the 1950s. The Lomé Convention actively contributed to promote a socialisation of the ACPs into the European model through the multiplication of group-to-group institutions which conferred a high visibility upon European institutions.[33] European aid programmes have also involved the dispensation of expertise in line with Brussels' own understanding of region-building. A most obvious legacy of these years is provided by the UEMOA and CEMAC treaties which were drawn by experts from the European Commission and patterned along the newly established European Economic and Monetary Union (EMU). The EU's economic trajectory, it should be conceded, seemed to offer an exemplary confirmation of the scenarios for economic integration (free trade area, customs union, common market and finally monetary union) that were suggested in the fifties and early sixties by influential economists.[34]

Given the extensive aid and expertise drawn from Europe, it is not really surprising that the RECs borrowed the idea that the deepening of economic integration would progress through transfers of sovereignty to a supranational entity. The AU's revised treaty also draws much of its inspiration from the EU's politico-institutional architecture, although the organisation is, in effect, operating on a strictly inter-governmental basis. Since 2005, the EU has also turned from model to mentor, as interactions between the EU and the AU were institutionalised, through the organisation of Commission to Commission meetings – now known as College to College (C2C) meetings – entrusted with reviewing the progress of the Joint Africa EU Strategic Partnership (JAES).

It does not fall within the ambit of this paper to provide a comprehensive review of the achievements and failings of regionalism in Africa. The topic is no longer ignored or side-tracked. Cohorts of experts, policy-makers and scholars monitor security and peace-keeping, while the 'defragmentation' of African markets generates active interest from both old and new players. The chequered process of negotiating the inter-regional EPAs with the EC has also contributed to an increase in public awareness and mobilisation within African civil society. Such problems as the simultaneous participation of states in several RECs, the heavy reliance of African regional institutions on external funding – recently illustrated by China's construction of the AU's new Addis Ababa headquarters – or the implementation deficit that affects policies agreed upon are widely discussed.[35]

Current assessments of regional economic integration in Africa, while celebrating Africa's transformation into a new frontier for international trade and investment, simultaneously stress that the continent remains a collection of "fragmented small economies" (Janneh, 2011). There is also a striking contrast between the dynamism of the so-called 'informal' trade and the quasi-irrelevance (11 per cent) of recorded intra-regional flows compared to what is being monitored in Europe (72 per cent) and Asia (52 per cent).[36] This reflects on the poor implementation of stated policies, but also on the limitations of a trade-driven approach to regional integration within regional economic communities and the future AEC.[37]

The establishment of Free Trade Areas (FTAs) and customs unions within the RECs was originally meant to have taken place within respectively 10 and 12 years following the adoption of the Abuja treaty in 1991. Two decades later, AMU, CENSAD and IGAD are nowhere near any progress towards establishing FTAs. In the Maghreb, member states of the AMU have not been able to meet for several years. In the Horn of Africa, IGAD is still primarily a political forum, while CENSAD is probably doomed to fade into oblivion after the eviction of its Libyan patron and financier, Muammar Ghaddafi. While ECOWAS, ECCAS and the EAC have formally announced the establishment of their FTAs, SADC is yet to achieve this objective despite the formal claim (on its website) that the FTA was 'launched' in 2008. At a time when the African economies have never been so integrated within the global economy, the regionalisation of markets and policies remains embryonic.

The EAC is the only regional economic grouping that has evolved from a FTA into a customs union. This should not, however, be considered as a forewarning of evolutions that are about to take place in the other groupings. The EAC is a much smaller (five) member-state organisation with a business oriented slant and, unlike the other groupings, an established record of cooperation and shared common services dating back to the colonial period. Kenya, mainland Tanzania and Uganda were initially included into an East Africa High Commission (EAHC), established in 1948 by the British to manage external defence, a common external tariff, a common currency and common services that covered an extensive range of issues and activities.[38]

In 1961, the EAHC was replaced by a new organization, the Common Services organization (EACSO) that maintained the common market and currency base, co-coordinated taxation and allocated resources from the distribution pool. Legislation on the matters entrusted to EACSO was passed by a regional parliament, the Central Legislative Assembly, which was less dependent upon the administration, but had little capacity for political initiative. Decisions were effectively adopted on an inter-governmental basis by triumvirates of ministers drawn from the different states or territories.

Dissatisfaction in Uganda and Tanzania over the distribution of the benefits of the customs union and common services meant that by 1965, all three states had issued their national currencies and the future of the CSO was threatened by the introduction of tariff barriers. In this context, the Treaty that established the East African Community in 1967 was a belated attempt at interrupting the fragmentation of the common market base of the CSO through the introduction of transfer-taxes that were meant to ensure equitable redistribution of the benefits drawn by the most industrialized country, namely Kenya. This new mechanism, however, amounted to tariff protection and became another subject of controversy. It would still take almost a decade until the EAC formally collapsed when, in 1977, member-states stopped paying their dues while Tanzania closed its border with Kenya.

The Arusha Treaty re-establishing the EAC was signed on 30 November 1999 by Tanzania, Kenya and Uganda, following a decade and a half of co-operative arrangements designed to harmonize monetary and fiscal policies, promote the restoration of a customs union, and establish common regulatory frameworks to attract investors. The treaty is particularly ambitious since it ultimately commits its signatories to the establishment of a 'Political Federation'.[39] Frustrated by the slow progress of integration within COMESA, private sector operators pressed repeatedly for the reestablishment of EAC, encouraged by new prospects for convergence due to pro-market economic reforms within all three states. By the time the heads of state of the EAC met in November 2004, co-ordination of national policies had already achieved significant progress in several areas, in conjunction with regional networking and institution (re-) building. Major institutions include the Summit, the Council of Ministers, the Secretariat (since 1996), the East African Assembly and the East African Court of Appeal (2001). Regional structures revitalised or newly established include the East African Business Council, the East African Development Bank, the Inter-University Council for East Africa (2000), the Lake Victoria Development Unit (2001), the East African Council for Science and Technology (2001), etc.

Lessons drawn from the pros and cons of the initial EAC, but also lingering representations of the region as a social and cognitive space and, above all, the ability of member-states and their bureaucracies to conceive economic integration as a 'common good' have sustained the build up of a momentum that, today, can appear to be credible as it plans for the establishment of a common currency by 2012. This capacity of the EAC to reinvent itself is in stark contrast with SACU's inability to do so. As a result, the oldest working customs union in Africa is being threatened by South Africa's declining interest for a regime (pooling and redistribution of the revenues) that has been breeding patronage and status quo preservation.

The achievements of the EAC are a reminder that the ability of regional organisations to implement intrusive institutional agendas presumes that member-states voluntarily concede a reduction of national prerogatives and territorial control. This postulates a capacity and willingness to do so, an issue that refers in fine to the production and implementation of 'public' policies that do not simply reflect upon the private interests of the ruler and his clients. It is the limited ability of some states to craft public policies and ensure the protection of their citizens that has prompted the increasing engagement of both the RECs and AU in conflict prevention, peace keeping initiatives and post conflict transitions. Accordingly, African regional institutions have, within the past decade, become increasingly engaged in the reconstruction of state society interactions. Nkrumah's once famous independence motto: "Seek ye first the political kingdom", remains as topical as ever, this time due to the growing engagement of regional organisation into conflict resolution within its member-states.

The limited capacity of African regional organisations to implement their ambitious integrationist agendas cannot be simply attributed to the existence or absence of supranational decision-making processes or to a lack of political will on the part of member-states. Thick institutional agendas contribute to exacerbate the adverse effects of the coexistence, within African regional and continental groupings, of thoroughly patrimonialised and predatory regimes along with states within which patrimonialism is capped and ring-fenced.[40] Procrastination over the dismantlement of tariff and non-tariff barriers despite formal commitments to do so by the state or its agents deserves to be understood in this broader context.

Endnotes

1   The Economist, 2011: 13; Invest AD, 2012

2   S. Ladd, (2012), "Emerging Africa expected to see rise in Investment", *IMF Survey*, 12 January.

3   Daniel C. Bach (2012), "Thick Institutionalism versus Lean Integration: New Regionalism in Africa", in Candice Moore, ed., *Regional Integration and Social Cohesion: A Missing Link?*, Frantfurt: Peter Lang, p. 91

4   Ibid, p.92.

5   Daniel C. Bach (2013), "Regionalism in Africa: Concepts and Context", in James J. Hentz (Ed.) *Routledge Handbook of African Security*, London: Routledge

6   Integration does not proceed from the transfer of sovereign competencies to a supranational entity, but from the continuation of arrangements dating back to the colonial period. At independence, the decision to continue pre-existing arrangements, meant that accession to international sovereignty excluded currency (franc CFA zone) or external tariff and customs (SACU) management. These remained entrusted to respectively France and South Africa (Bach 2005:137–148).

7   Engel and Porto (2013), "The African Union and African Security" in James J. Hentz (Ed.) *Routledge Handbook of African Security*, London: Routledge

8   The CA prescribes that the AU has "the right . . . to intervene in a Member State pursuant to a decision of the Assembly in respect of grave circumstances, namely war crimes, genocide and crimes against humanity" (art. 4 section h). See also, the extensive discussion of R2P in Chapter 4.

9   Abdoulie Janneh (2011), Opening remarks by Abdoulie Janneh UN UnderSecretary-General and Executive Secretary of ECA, Addis Ababa, 22 November 2011, At: <http://www.trademarksa.org/news/africa-trade-forum2011-speech-abdoulie-janneh-0>.; see also ECA, AU, ADB 2010

10 ECA, AU, ADB 2010, pp. 1–4

11 Daniel C. Bach (2013), p. 186.

12 "The State of Regional Integration in East Africa: Perspectives on Model, Pace and Future Trajectory", Workshop of the Institute of Regional Integration and Development, The Catholic University of Eastern Africa, Nairobi (Kenya), 26 September 2012.

13   Bach 2012, p.100.

14   Ibid.

15   Tijani Alou, Mahaman (2011), "Monitoring the neopatrimonial state on a dayto-day basis: politicians, customs officials and traders in Niger", in Daniel C., Bach & Mamoudou, Gazibo (eds.), *The neopatrimonial state in Africa and Beyond*, Oxford: Routledge, pp. 142–54

16   Sally Healy, (2011), *Hostage to Conflict: Prospects for Building Regional Economic Cooperation in the Horn of Africa*, A Chatham House Report, Chatham House, London: November.

17   Daniel C. Bach (2013), p. 188.

18   Invest AD (2012), *Into Africa, Institutional Investor Intentions to 2016*, Doha: Invest AD & London: Economist Intelligence Unit, January At <http://investad.com/reports/intoafrica.html>.

19   Daniel C. Bach (2013), p. 188.

20   Ibid.

21   Cristiano D'Orsi, "Why barriers to a pan-African passport may be insurmountable", *The Conversation,* July 19, 2016, https://theconversation.com/why-barriers-to-a-pan-african-passport-may-be-insurmountable-62602

22   Daniel C. Bach (2012), p.92.

23   Ibid.

24   Hettne, Björn and Fredrik, Söderbaum (2000), "Theorising the Rise of Regionness", *New Political Economy*, Vol. 5, No. 3, pp. 457-74.

25   Andrew W. Axline, (1977), "Underdevelopment, Dependence and Integration: The Politics of Regionalism in the Third world", *International Organization*, Vol. XXXI, No. 1, p. 83.

26   Higgot, Richard (1995), "Economic co operation in the Asia Pacific: A theoretical comparison with the European Union", *Journal of European Public Policy*, Vol. 2, No. 3, pp. 361-63.

27   Alex Warleigh-Lack, Nick Robinson, Ben Rosamond (eds.) (2010), *New regionalism and the European Union*, Oxford: Routledge.

28 Daniel Bach (2011), "Organisations régionales et régionalisation: crise en Europe, essor au-delà", in Bertrand, Badie & Dominique, Vidal (eds.), *Nouveaux acteurs, nouvelle donne, L'État du monde 2012*, Paris: La Découverte, p. 29-38.

29 Helge Hveem (1999), "Political Regionalism: Master or Servant of Economic Internationalization?", in Björn, Hettne; Andras, Inotai & Osvaldo, Sunkel (eds.), *Globalism and the New Regionalism*, London: Macmillan, pp. 85-115.

30 Daniel Bach(2005), "Integration through Hysteresis: SACU in a Comparative and Contextual Perspective", in Hansohm, Dirk; Breytenbach, Willie et al. (eds.), *Monitoring Regional Integration in Southern Africa*, Yearbook 5, Windhoek: Namibian Economic Policy Research Unit (NEPRU), p. 135-48.

31 The notion is borrowed from Paul Collier which used it to describe the commitment to domestic or external "institutions which protect public assets from depletion, prevent inflationary money printing, prevent corruption, protect socially productive groups from exploitation, and enforce contracts"(Collier, 1991 340-1). The concept applied to the discussion of macroeconomic policies and was popularised through discussions of the performance of the CFA franc monetary unions.

32 The CA prescribes that the AU has "the right ... to intervene in a Member State pursuant to a decision of the Assembly in respect of grave circumstances, namely war crimes, genocide and crimes against humanity" (art. 4 section h).

33 Joint institutions still include the ACP-EU Council of Ministers, the EU-ACP Committee of Ambassadors, and the Joint Consultative Assembly composed of an equal number of ACP parliamentarians and representatives from the European Parliament.

34 Bela Balassa (1961), *The Theory of Economic Integration*, Homewood: R.D. Irwin.

35 ECA, AU & ADB:2010

36 ECA, AU & ADB, 2010: 1-4

37 Sean Woolfrey (2012), "The rationale for boosting intra-african trade", *Tralac*, 1 February. At <http://www.tralac.org/2012/02/01/the-rationale-forboosting-intra-african-trade/>.

38 Arthur Hazelwood (1975), *Economic Integration: the East African Experience*, London: Heinemann., p. 28; Common services covered activities such as customs, excise and income tax as well as transport and communication services

(including the East African Airways Corporation), applied research, statistical data collection and higher education (at Makerere College).

39 The Arusha Treaty alternatively refers alternatively to the formation of a "political federation" or to a "federation of the partner states" See Preamble, Art. 5, Para. 2; Art. 11, Para. 3 and Art. 123, para. 1 (EAC: 2011).

40 Daniel C. Bach and Mamoudou Gazibo (Eds) (2012), *Neopatrimonialism in Africa and Beyond*, Abingdon :Routledge

Chapter - 5

Africa and the World: AU's Interface

T he continental body has a dual role of forging unity among its member states and advocating their interests internationally.[1] During its first ten years of existence the AU's role as an international actor has been complicated by the difficulty of promoting consensus among African states and then maintaining that consensus in the face of often divergent national interests. The Africa Group at the UN General Assembly works to forge consensus on key issues of Pan-African interest, such as development, trade, debt cancellation, infectious diseases, small arms and light weapons, nuclear, chemical and biological weapons, climate negotiations, trans-national crime prevention, and the election of Africans to various UN activities and bodies.[2]

This chapter has looked at African geo-strategic reality under globalization and has tried to observe AU factor in the interrelatiships between Africa and the extra-regional powers, including the dominant and emerging ones. The thrust of this chapter has been placed on traditional and emerging actors and their engagements with the AU.

AU-UN Interface on Global Governance

In March 2005, the AU issued a declaration known as 'The Common African Position on the Proposed Reform of the United Nations: the Ezulwini Consensus', which highlighted issues pertaining to HIV/AIDS and security, poverty, debt, environmental degradation, trade negotiations, the responsibility to protect, peacekeeping, and peace building.[3] In addition, the AU issued a position on UN reform and in particular on the reform of the Security Council by noting that 'in 1945, when the UN was formed, most of Africa was not represented and that in 1963, when the first reform took place, Africa was represented but was not in a particularly strong position.'[4] It continues that 'Africa's goal is to be fully represented in all the decision-making organs of the UN, particularly in the Security Council'.[5] The Common Position enumerates what 'full representation' of Africa in the Security Council means by demanding 'not less than two permanent seats with all the prerogatives and privileges of permanent membership including the right to veto' and 'five non-permanent seats.'[6]

On paper, the AU was attempting to establish and maintain a common position, but in practice some countries, including South Africa, broke ranks with the Ezulwini Consensus and sought ways to ascend individually to become permanent members of the Security Council. This in effect undermined efforts to demonstrate African 'unity of purpose'. It was not the first time this had happened: time and again African countries have shown that they are unlikely to vote as a collective on matters before, or pertaining to, the Security Council – a clear indication that member states are not respecting the AU as a norm entrepreneur. Governments generally tend to adopt positions that best serve their interests, or positions that enable them to receive certain benefits from more powerful countries that 'pick and choose' which countries they want to work with.[7]

Malawi's move to deny President Omar Al Bashir of Sudan access to the AU Summit, due to be hosted in Lilongwe in July 2012, is a case in point. Explaining Malawi's reasons for taking this stance, President Joyce Banda stated that her country's commitment to its donors, notably the United Kingdom as the largest bilateral contributor, and its desire to uphold the ICC's Rome Statute, would not allow it to host Bashir, an alleged war criminal. The AU Commission subsequently took the decision to relocate the Summit to Addis Ababa, rather than submit to Banda's injunction. The logic of national self-interest and political realism can thus be seen to have prevailed among African countries, as well as member states at the UN.[8]

AU and the EU

The Africa focus of the EU goes back to the adoption of the Treaty of Rome and the establishment of the European Economic Community (EEC) in 1958. Special association status was then granted to the (yet to become independent) French and Belgian colonies in sub-Saharan Africa. The outcome was the incorporation of specific provisions in Title IV of the Treaty establishing the EEC.[9] The United Kingdom's accession to the EEC in 1973 was followed by negotiations towards the enlargement of the group of associated states. In February 1975, the adoption of the Lomé Convention signalled the formation of the group of African, Caribbean and Pacific (ACP) states, a grouping that subsequently expanded so as to eventually include all 48 sub-Saharan African countries.

The Lomé Convention had the rather ambitious objective to promote an integrated approach to development. A non-reciprocal trade regime conferred totally free access to the EU market on all ACP exports of manufactured products and on 95 percent of agricultural products. This placed the developing economies of sub-Saharan Africa at the apex of the pyramid of EU trade preferences to developing economies.[10] Lomé also inaugurated policy instruments designed to temper the fluctuations in the export prices of agricultural and mining products. Development aid was committed on five-year terms and went along with the introduction of 'comanagement' procedures. In order to promote the values of partnership and encourage North-South dialogue, group-to-group institutions were established. They included the ACP-EU Council of Ministers, the EU-ACP Committee of Ambassadors, and the Joint Consultative Assembly composed of an equal number of ACP parliamentarians and representatives from the European Parliament. Current references to the Africa-EU strategic partnership are rooted in the history of these group-to-group institutions.

Lomé negotiations were conducted in the wake of the oil boom (and embargo) of September 1973 at a time when Europeans were particularly concerned at ensuring stable access to oil and other strategic minerals. This particular conjuncture would also leave its mark on the outcome of the negotiations. Indeed, the set of instruments and procedures that were then adopted was meant to offer a model for the reordering of North-South relations. With the failure of the Paris and Cancun conferences on a new North-South international order, Lomé progressively became the symbol of unfulfilled promises and differing expectations. Excepting Mauritius, the ACP's trade regime had failed to stimulate a diversification of economies away from the export of unprocessed commodities. Despite the preferential access given to ACP exports, these were losing ground on the EU market due to competition from South-East Asian and Latin American exporters.[11]

In addition to this, the Convention's parity-based institutional architecture and the context of the cold war stimulated collective clientelism.[12] Reforming relations with sub-Saharan Africa nonetheless remained a taboo subject until the early 1990s. By then, the fall of communism in Europe, the EU's changing priorities due to the prospects for enlargement by another 10 new member states, and the conclusion of the General Agreement on Tariffs and Trade (GATT) negotiations suddenly transformed the review of Lomé into a priority. On 23 June 2000, after half a decade of semi-official debates and a two-year renegotiation process, the EU and 77 ACP countries signed the Cotonou Partnership Agreement (CPA) that superseded the Lomé Convention. Cotonou purported to provide the roadmap towards a new and original inter-hemispheric partnership based on subscription to common political norms, trade reciprocity, and the conclusion of Economic Partnership Agreements (EPAs).[13] These were meant to promote free trade between the EU and six regional groupings, four of them in sub-Saharan Africa.

The Cotonou Agreement departs from Lomé insofar as it inserts into a broader and generic approach the specific treatment previously granted to ACP countries. Human rights, democratisation and the rule of law are defined (Article 9) as an 'essential element' that may result, in the case of 'particularly serious and flagrant violation', in aid and trade sanctions. The streamlining process that underscores Cotonou also stems from the end of the GATT/World Trade Organisation (WTO) waiver that allowed trade concessions to ACP countries until December 2007. WTO compliance now requires the progressive liberalisation of trade between Europe and Africa over a 12-year period so as to achieve completion by 2020.[14]

Two sets of related international developments have further eroded the value of past EU trade concessions to sub-Saharan Africa. First, the benefits that ACP countries used to draw from their exemption from the restraints imposed on Asian textile and clothing exports have lost their value with the termination of the quantitative restrictions imposed by Multi-Fibre Arrangements (MFAs) in December 2004. In addition to this, adverse rulings by WTO arbitration panels have dented the preferential treatment that special EU protocols used to offer to ACP exports for sugar, bananas, and beef. By the mid-2000s, South Africa already constituted the only exception to a pattern of dereliction that permeated trade and investment flows between Europe and sub-Saharan Africa — in 2004, South Africa alone accounted for 42 per cent of EU trade with sub-Saharan Africa.

The 3rd Africa-EU Summit, held in Tripoli in November 2010, was poorly attended and did not ignite the interest of the European and African press. This is not altogether surprising since implementation of the objectives assigned to the first Action Plan of the JAES has been hampered by poor levels of involvement and weak mobilization on the part of both AU and EU member states. As a result, the JAES — almost exclusively funded by the European Commission—has become heavily dependent on the dynamics of interactions between the EU and AU commissions; and this has, in turn, generated specific problems due to the wide disparity between their resources and powers. Poor mobilisation of member states has been compounded by an all encompassing agenda, the absence of clearly stated priorities, and the problems of co-ordination with the ENP or the RECs. Within the EU Commission, the value and implications of claiming to 'treat Africa as one' have not been properly assessed either.[15]

Much of the problem also seems to relate to the incapacity of the EU to speak as one, an area where little progress has been achieved despite the reorganisation of the EU's external policy instruments. The outcome is a 'construction' of Africa that is bound to appeal to the two commissions, but remains oblivious to the diversity of interests and weak enforcement capacity — as signified by the politics of overlapping membership within regional groupings and their poor performance as 'building blocs' since the adoption of the Abuja Plan of Action in 1991.[16]

The EU's stated ambition to treat the African continent as a strategic partner coexist with policy orientations that negate this objective as these contribute to the treatment of sub-Saharan Africa as a 'distant abroad' of Europe. This repeatedly points to the need for the EU and its member states to clarify and co-ordinate what Europe's interests in sub-Saharan Africa are, or should be. Today, the question arises even more dramatically in North Africa where, since early 2011, the demise of authoritarian regimes in Tunisia and Egypt has ushered in demands for freedom, democracy, and social justice across the Middle East. The recent prognosis that the so-called 'Beijing Consensus', based on the rise of virtuous interactions between capitalism and authoritarian rule, would 'dominate the ... [twenty-first] century',[17] has suddenly come in for some serious empirical reassessment.[18]

North Africa's unanticipated and domestically rooted demands for democracy are also brutally exposing the coexistence of the ideals of partnership, brought forward by the EU's JAES and ENP initiatives, with a 'Brussels Consensus' that is largely driven by the specific priorities of EU member states. In a nutshell, the consensus is a trade-off that minimises violations of democracy and human rights, while valuing trade liberalisation, the securitisation of Europe's external frontiers, and political stability. The ambitions assigned to the 'strategic partnership' with Africa are yet to be reconciled with the substantive interests subsumed under the equation of the 'Brussels Consensus.'[19]

Enlargement was frequently described as the foreign policy of Europe during the 1990s and early 2000s. Since the mid-2000s, it is the securitisation of Europe's external frontiers and 'near abroad' that permeates converging and increasingly high-profile foreign policy initiatives. For the countries of the Maghreb, prospects for an improvement in their access to Europe and its market have become explicitly linked to their readiness to control their shores and land-borders. The extension of controls along the Sahel-Saharan borderlines and the intra-regional boundaries of the Maghreb states also stems from the post-9/11 security overlay, stimulated by the terrorist attacks in Casablanca and Madrid and weariness that such radical Islamist groups as Al-Qaida au Maghreb Islamique (AQMI) may transform the southern fringes of the Maghreb and the Sahel into a sanctuary.[20]

The implications of this trend for sub-Saharan migration flows have been broad ranging. By the turn of the new millennium, sub-Saharan Africans accounted for the bulk of trans-national migrants seeking opportunities for illicit crossovers from Morocco, Tunisia, or Libya.[21] Impoverished and often stranded, these migrants have borne the full brunt of the increasingly active involvement of the Maghreb countries in the management of European asylum and migration policies. In Tunisia, as in Morocco, Algeria and Libya, this meant by the mid-2000s a tightening of 'controls on the southern borders of the Maghreb states [and] ... rules on the entry, residence and employment of foreigners' in an overall context characterized by problems 'related to the rights (and lack of rights)' of migrants and stricter 'border controls at points of departure to Europe'.[22] Such readiness to regulate migration flows has also contributed to entrench sub-Saharan Africa as a European 'distant abroad'.

During this period, the EU's announcement of a new initiative, the European Neighbourhood Policy (ENP), also created an institutional basis for dissociating interactions with North Africa from those with sub-Saharan Africa. Launched in 2004, the ENP is meant to promote a relationship between the EU and its immediate neighbours that will 'ultimately resemble the close political and economic links currently enjoyed with the European Economic Area' (EU, 2003, 15). This process — popularised through the formula 'everything but institutions' — involves the conclusion, as a preliminary step, of specific action plans. These may, in turn, open the way to 'mobility packages' designed to provide better access to the EU for those countries willing to co-operate on re-admission, irregular migration, and border management.[23]

The process also involves participation in joint monitoring patrols and common policing operations across the Mediterranean, as well as access to material and financial assistance through police training, presence of liaison officers, and so on.[24] The expectation is that responsibility for the management of these issues can be delegated to a network of non-EU countries, mostly from its immediate neighbourhood. By contrast, sub-Saharan African countries do not benefit from any linkage between EU visa facilitation and re-admission agreements. Indeed, the EU considers that the link that Cotonou's Article 13 establishes between migration issues and development provides an adequate basis for the conclusion of supplementary bilateral re-admission agreements between selected ACP countries and EU member states.[25]

As the Lisbon Summit was about to be convened in December 2007, EU member states acknowledged that, despite restrictive immigration policies, large numbers of illegal migrants still reached Europe. But it was also noted that Europe would require an additional 20mn often highly-skilled workers by 2025. Debates accordingly shifted towards the adoption of common policies and EU legislation designed to enhance the mobility of highly-skilled or seasonal labour across the Mediterranean, while countering an avalanche of unskilled migrations through increased operational cooperation between member states. Since then, the adoption of the European Pact on Immigration and Asylum in December 2008 has confirmed an approach that looks at immigration policies through the prism of 'control first', but for highly-skilled migrants now eligible for an EU blue card scheme.

The priority assigned to border security and trade liberalisation has also prompted the EU and its member states to disregard violations of democratic and human rights by authoritarian regimes in the Maghreb. Accordingly, in May 2010, the EU Commission for Enlargement and the European Neighbourhood Policy had no hesitation in depicting Tunisia as 'an important and reliable partner' and 'an economic pioneer among the European Union neighbours' (ENPI Info Centre, 2010). The responsible EU Commissioner also announced that the 8th EU-Tunisia Association Council was about to 'set up an ad hoc group to work on a roadmap which would lead us to … [an] advanced status. That advanced status will be focussing …

[on] more intense political dialogue, legislative approximation, [and] a deep and comprehensive free trade agreement' (ENPI Info Centre, 2010). By July 2010, the Zine el Abidine Ben Ali regime apparently felt confident enough to amend Tunisia's criminal code so as to forbid contacts between Tunisian human rights organizations and European institutions.[26]

The year 2005 was dubbed the 'Year of Africa' due to the continent's designation as a special issue on the agenda of the G8 Gleneagles Summit. The multiplication of initiatives in Europe and North America that focused on the African continent meant that, by the middle of that year, a cathartic atmosphere surrounded the 'Live 8' concerts and the flurry of other activities sponsored by non-governmental organisations (NGOs). These events and the summit itself also marked the highpoint of a vision of Africa that stressed humanitarianism and moralistic imperatives. The situation on the continent, described earlier by British Prime Minister Tony Blair as 'a scar on the conscience of the world',[27] was perceived as an emblematic expression of the legacy of colonialism and the pitfalls of globalisation. Under strong pressure from public opinion across Europe and the US, the G8 summit subsequently announced plans towards a comprehensive 'Africa Action Plan' that would combine debt relief, increased official development assistance (ODA), infrastructure rehabilitation, and a sustained commitment to poverty alleviation on the continent.

In the US, as in Europe, emphasis on humanitarianism often went along with downgraded assessments of the geo-strategic and economic stakes associated with the African continent. The Africa Report that was released in December 2005 by the US Council on Foreign Relations was, therefore, groundbreaking in several respects (Council on Foreign Relations, 2005). While celebrating the 'noble commitments' and 'humanitarian impulses' that went along with the Gleneagles Summit, its authors made a case for redefining policy orientations that would, as they put it, go 'beyond humanitarianism' and 'charity-inspired blueprints'. Two years later, EU Commissioner for Development Louis Michel (2007) similarly denounced 'Afro-pessimism and the "caritative" or even paternalistic overtones' of past relations, while committing the EU to a new and strategic relationship with Africa.[28]

It is against this background that the Second Africa-Europe Summit was held in Lisbon in December 2007. The summit was designed to promote and endorse a radical shift in EU-Africa relations. It also epitomised feelings that, as had been the case in the wake of the 1973 oil crisis, a transformation of the rapports de force (power relations) between Europe and ACP countries was on the way. The decision to convene the Lisbon Summit followed Europe's acceptance that Zimbabwe's Robert Mugabe be invited, despite persistent opposition from British Prime Minister Gordon Brown. The EU's decision to back-track on this issue barely concealed the view that the success of the Second Forum for China-Africa Co-operation (FOCAC) held in Beijing a year earlier should not be left unmatched. The attendance of 80 states was, in this sense, a huge success. The Lisbon summit also reflected on the ability of Europeans and Africans to discuss publicly the substance of their relationship, in sharp contrast to the smooth flow of speeches, echoed by uncritical press comments, during the Focac summit. At the urging of two particularly active personalities, European Commissioner Louis Michel and AU President Alpha Oumar Konaré, the Lisbon Summit also announced a partnership and a 'new era' for Europe-Africa relations through the adoption of a Joint Africa-EU Strategy (JAES).

The objective of the JAES and its first Action Plan (2008-2010) is the establishment of a much more overtly political relationship than had been the case through Lomé, Cotonou, or the Euro-Mediterranean Partnership (EU, 2005). To this effect, the thematic areas earmarked in the JAES range from aid and development — trade, regional integration, infrastructure, and the Millennium Development Goals (MDGs)—to peace and security, democratic governance, and migration. The holistic ambition of the agendas is also signalled by the inclusion of energy and climate change, along with science, information and communications technology, and space exploration. To promote these partnerships, the JAES stress the importance of a dialogue based on the principle of a 'partnership of equals', an approach designed to be a radical departure from past representations and interactions. A closely related ambition of the JAES is to 'treat Africa as one', namely to contribute to overcoming the incoherencies resulting from the patchwork of European instruments and agreements focused on specific areas of the continent. While a specific Trade and Development Co-operation Agreement (TDCA) ties the EU to South Africa, the rest of sub-Saharan Africa along with the Pacific and Caribbean countries (ACP) are signatories to the Cotonou Agreement. In North Africa, two sets of agreement coexist: the Euro-Mediterranean Partnership and the European Neighbourhood Policy. The JAES seeks to overcome this fragmentation through the promotion of a global framework for the treatment of EU-Africa relations.[29]

The regular contacts between the Commission of the AU and the European Commission — a model turned into a mentor in many respects — have come to symbolise the ambition to 'treat Africa as one' and to transcend purely development oriented agendas.[30] Initiated in 2005, the Commission-to-Commission meetings have sustained the momentum for the construction of EU-Africa political agendas. Already at the 4th Ministerial Meeting of the African and European Troikas,9 held in Luxembourg on 11 April 2005, the President of the European Council stressed that 'the EU considers the AU as its main counterpart within the EU-Africa dialogue, being understood that Morocco remains associated in a pragmatic way'.[31]

Six months later, on 12 October 2005, the first AU-EU Commission-to-Commission Meeting was convened in Brussels on the same day the European Commission's proposals for an 'EU Strategy for Africa' (CEC, 2005) were adopted. The event brought together the chairmen of the two institutions, as well as 8 AU and 19 EU commissioners. A joint working plan was adopted, along with the strengthening of institutional ties, the pursuit of 'regular political and institutional dialogue', and 'twinning programmes' between commissioners entrusted with similar portfolios (CEC, 2005). Since 2008, commission-to-commission meetings, known today as 'college-to-college' meetings (C2Cs), were convened once a year. Besides monitoring the implementation of the JAES, C2C meetings also offer an avenue for specific activities on bilateral co-operation between the two commissions. It is on such grounds that the joint appointment by the European Council and the EU Commission of a Special Representative of the EU to the AU was announced in December 2007 — a nomination that anticipated the implementation of the Lisbon Treaty.[32]

Emphasis on 'partnership' and the holistic vision embedded in the JAES — meant to go 'beyond development', 'beyond Africa', and 'beyond institutions' [33] — have resulted in the establishment of an impressive array of structures. Political dialogue and (since September 2008) monitoring the implementation of the JAES also feature on the agenda of the biannual meetings of the EU-Africa ministerial troikas. Other significant structures established to promote the objectives of the JAES include EU and AU Implementation Teams (ITs), as well as the eight Joint Expert Groups (JEGs) that are to co-ordinate, prepare for, and implement the priorities of the 'Action Plan'. The outcome is a mix of institutions and processes designed to promote partnerships on an inter-continental and multi-tier basis — namely, between member states, EU and AU commissions, regional parliaments, civil society organisations (CSOs), and so on. Legal and financial constraints, as well as poor commitment on the part of EU and AU member states, have considerably dampened the bold objectives initially stated. The JAES and its action plan is not a legally agreed framework, unlike the TDCA, the CPA, or the ENP action plans. The structures established under the JAES and its action plan is yet to overcome the effects of the coexistence of overlapping agreements and institutions. The AU, entrusted with particularly high expectations by the European Council, is still handicapped by problems of governance and funding. Interaction with the Regional Economic Communities (RECs) and their ability to operate as 'building blocks' continue to be hampered by problems of overlapping memberships and uneven enforcement of commonly agreed decisions.

However, the ability of the JEGs to bring in CSOs and generate new ideas has been severely constrained — they are not entitled to take new policy initiatives or decisions, unlike what was initially expected.[34] This means, for instance, that they still have no capacity to impact on the ongoing negotiations towards the conclusion of EPAs. In addition, and unlike what African countries initially anticipated, no specific funding has been earmarked to support the ambitious agendas of these partnerships. The action plans, the European Commission has been arguing, are designed to stimulate political dialogue, but the resulting initiatives should not undercut the functioning of existing instruments for EU-Africa development cooperation.[35]

Work within the JEGs is heavily dependent on the dynamism and expertise of their self-appointed members, chairs and cochairs. Moreover, the AU Commission does not have adequate human resources to monitor work within each of the eight partnerships. As a result, the achievements associated with the JAES often have a bearing more on institution-building than on capacity-building, regional and sub-regional organisations, the 'need to review the JEG mandate and guidelines', and the mobilisation of 'adequate funds and human/technical resources'.[36] Beyond the usual precautionary formulations, what was and remains at stake is the elusive capacity of the JAES to go beyond.

The 13th Meeting of the Africa-EU Ministerial Troika, held in Addis Ababa on 14 October 2009, characteristically called for a 'fundamental review' accompanied by 'significant changes', but the draft joint options paper adopted six months later opted instead for excluding changes from the text of the joint strategy. The current priority areas of the action plan, it was decided, ought to remain unchanged. Attention should rather be given to enhanced implementation, further dialogue, and more involvement by JAES actors. Other suggestions included fuller participation and interaction with African hat such existing instruments as the CPA, the ENP, or the Euro-Mediterranean Partnership already offer.

Until 2007, the European Commission (EC) did not comment publicly on China's fast increasing engagement with Africa through trade, aid, investment and high profile politico- diplomatic initiatives. By October 2005, a kind of business-as-usual approach prevailed in Brussels as the Commission prepared the release of its new strategy for Euro-African relations.[37] The communication that was eventually released acknowledged China's rising importance to Africa, through a tangential and low key reference that carefully steered away from drawing any conclusion:

> China merits special attention given its economic weight and political influence ... Despite radical domestic changes, the country has retained links with different African countries which are now attracted by China's trading potential. Especially for oil- and commodity-dependent countries, China represents a substantial and continued source of financial income, mostly outside the traditional development and governance frameworks.[38]

A few weeks later, the Council of the EU adopted a statement that endorsed the strategy recommended by the EC in its communication.[39] This time, however, no reference was made to China, a silence that contrasted with the extensive policy debates that, within the EC, in the European parliament and among member states, focused on China's emergence as a global actor. Each in their own way, the EC and the Council of the EU seemed unable or unwilling to address the implications of China and India's rising interactions with Africa and increasing significance in the hierarchy of global governance.

A year and a half later, in May 2007, the EC called for a rejuvenated EU–Africa strategic partnership, while noting that China's ability to 'rapidly emerge ... as Africa's third most important trade partner' would mean that 'if the EU wants to remain a privileged partner and make the most of its relations with Africa, it must be willing to reinforce and in some areas reinvent the current relationship – institutionally, politically and culturally'.[40] A few weeks academic and think-tank experts, civil society representatives and businessmen originating from China, Africa as well as Europe to discuss 'how the relations between the three actors can be brought into play to yield the best results for a win–win partnership around an African agenda'.[41] In his inaugural speech, Louis Michel, the EC Commissioner for Development and Humanitarian Aid, made a plea for the establishment of a triangular partnership, after stressing that 'we are competitors, but we are also partners and Africa must benefit from a reinforced relationship among ourselves and not suffer from it'.[42] Concrete steps designed to translate the political dialogue initiated in Brussels into cooperation initiatives included suggestions of a visit of the European Commissioner for Development to China and the possible invitation of China to the Euro-African summit of Lisbon.

The identification of areas suited for an EU-China 'partnership' over Africa was yet to translate into tangible results by January 2008. As Michel announced his intention to visit Beijing in March, he was pressed by journalists to clarify what interest China would find in committing itself to such a venture. The EU Commissioner answered that Beijing could secure 'though cooperation with Europe', a new 'credibility' to pursue its investment strategy'. Michel added that he believed that African elites were increasingly aware of the rise of Chinese interest in Africa, and that 'this will inevitably provoke reactions…Idyllic relations between Africa and China, are bound to end', he concluded.[43]

Prospects for a partnership with China were also being discussed at a time when protests aroused by the EU's Economic Partnership Agreements did not show any sign of weakening within Africa. By the beginning of 2008, President Abdulaye Wade of Senegal, also the leader of one the two African countries where democratic governance had gone uninterrupted since independence, was still one of the chief exponents of criticism of the EU templates, deftly capitalized on the issue domestically, while hammering in international fora and media that the EU 'should practice what it preaches', with respect to the translation of financial pledges into effective commitment and the emulation of (China's) 'best' practices. Wade's widely circulated phillippics targetted the 'West' in general and the EU in particular:

> China's approach to our needs is simply better adapted than the slow and sometimes patronising post-colonial approach of European investors, donor organisatins and non-governmental organisations…. With direct aid, credit lines and reasonable contracts, China has helped African nations to build infrastructure projects in record time... I

am a firm believer in good governance and the rule of law. But when bureaucracy and senseless red tape impede our ability to act...African leaders have an obligation to opt for swifter solutions. I achieved more in my one hour meeting with President Hu Jintao in an executive suite at my hotel in Berlin during the recent [2007] G8 meeting in Heiligendamm than I did during the entire, orchestrated meeting of world leaders at the summit... ... For the price of one European vehicle, a Senegalese can purchase two Chinese cars. ...[W] estern complaints about China's slow pace in adopting democratic reform cannot obscure the fact that the Chinese are more competitive, less bureaucratic and more adept at business in Africa than their critics..... If Europe does not want to provide funding for African infrastructure – it pledged $15bn under the Cotonou Agreement eight years ago – the Chinese are ready to take up the task, more rapidly and at less cost. Not just Africa but the west itself has much to learn from China.[44]

AU and the US

The African Growth Opportunity Act (AGOA) was signed into law in May 2000 by the President of the USA. The Act offers tangible incentives for African countries to continue their efforts to open their economies and build free markets. It is the most bilateral access to the U.S. market available to any country or region with which the United States does not have a free Trade Agreement. It supports U.S. business by encouraging reform of Africa's economic and commercial regimes, which will build stronger markets and more effective partners with U.S. firms. Since its establishment, AGOA has gone through three amendments; AGOA II in 2002, which substantially expanded preferential access for imports from beneficiary African countries; AGOA III, which provides for an Acceleration Act, extends preferential access for imports from beneficiary countries until September 2015 and the African Investment Incentive Act (AGOA), referred to as "AGOA IV". The legislation extends the third country fabric provision for an additional five years, from September 2007 until September 2012; adds an abundant supply provision, designates certain denim articles as being in abundant supply; and allows lesser developed beneficiary African countries export certain textile articles under AGOA.

An AGOA Implementation Subcommittee of the Trade Policy Staff Committee (TPSC) was established to implement AGOA. Among the most important implementation issues are the following: Determination of country eligibility; Determination of the products eligible for zero tariff under expansion of the Generalized System of preferences (GSP); Determination of compliance with the conditions for apparel benefits; Establishment of the U.S.-Sub-Saharan Africa Trade and Economic Forum; and Provisions for technical assistance to held countries qualify for benefits. Taking into account that this cooperation is governed by an Act of the United States Congress and it is bilateral in nature, AGOA is not considered within the context of the African Union's Strategic Partnerships. The African Union aims to develop proper partnership with the U.S. to reflect the on-going Strategic Engagement between the two sides, including AGOA.[45]

In August 2006, the United States became the first non-African country to establish a separate diplomatic mission to the African Union. The current U.S. Ambassador to the AU, Michael Battle, pledged to support AU efforts to "advance democracy and a free press, strengthen electoral systems, promote peace and security and advance AU efforts to get African leaders and civil society to promote and above all, to 'internalize' universal values of human rights, good governance, and rule of law." Of the total U.S. aid to Africa in 2008-an estimated $5.2 billion-no funds were specifically allocated to the African Union; rather, funds were funnelled to peacekeeping missions and AU-supported programs such as the Comprehensive Africa Agricultural Development Program and the New Partnership for Africa's Development. "U.S. support to the AU is ad hoc, crisis-driven, vulnerable to raids from other budget lines, and uneven from year-to-year," Cooke reported to the Senate in 2005. [46]

The United States does support peacekeeping in Africa, but such aid is allocated on a case-by-case basis. In 2008, $96.4 million went toward the Global Peace Operations Initiative (GPOI), a portion of which supports the African Contingency Operations Training and Assistance program (ACOTA). According to the U.S. Africa Command, ACOTA is designed "to improve African ability to respond quickly to crises by providing selected militaries with the training and equipment required to execute humanitarian or peace support operations." The FY2009 budget include a request of $106.2 million for the GPOI, with an estimated $80 million going toward African security assistance. Between 2006 and 2008, the United States sent $908 million to the UN/AU peacekeeping force in Darfur (the State Department requested close to $209 million in the FY2009 budget). The United States has given over $150 million to the AU peacekeeping mission in Somalia, and in August 2009 U.S. Secretary of State Hillary Clinton vowed additional assistance. The United States "would very much like to see a robust African Union," said Collins, but the State Department "has never been able to construct a coherent policy on what to do about Africa." Instead, he said, it continues to supply money to individual countries that benefit its interests, rather than giving more substantial funding to a regional body like the AU.[47]

In August 2014 America hosted the first US-Africa Summit at Washington DC which saw nearly 50 African head of States discussing multiple themes and utilising the summit as a platform to foster stronger US-Africa relations. The summit had an intention to build on the progress made since the US President Barack Obama's trip to Africa in 2013, advance the administration's focus on trade and investment in Africa, and highlight America's commitment to Africa's security, its democratic development, and its people. When America elected its first African-American President, the African continent was hopeful of renewing its relationship with America and forming stronger ties. But the Obama foreign policy has been largely focussed towards the other parts of the world, primarily Asia, resulting to its policies towards the African continent taking a back seat. This summit has been seen as one of the major initiatives of the Obama administration towards the African continent and being the first US President to hold the largest event with the African head of states and governments.[48]

The US Strategy towards the Sub Saharan Africa elevates two efforts that will be critical to the future of Africa: strengthening democratic institutions and boosting broad-based economic growth, including through trade and investment. The four pillars of this strategy are: strengthen democratic institutions, spur economic growth, trade and investment, advance peace and security and promote opportunity and development. The US-Africa Summit is historic purely because of the vision envisioned by the present US president and hosting a track one dialogue with almost the all the various head of states or governments (excluding Zimbabwe, Sudan, Eritrea, and Central African Republic), commencing a new era in its relationship with the African continent.[49]

The broader theme of the summit was 'Investing in the Next Generation', with emphasis given on ways through which the government can unlock the potential of the future generation of Africa. Though the previous presidents have worked tremendously for Africa with initiatives like African

Growth and Opportunity Act (AGOA), President's Emergency Plan for Aids Relief (PEPFAR) and Millennium Challenge Corporation (MCC), President Obama tried to synergize the US-Africa relations with an outlook towards the future by discussing various themes with the African leaders under one roof. In 2010 his administration launched 'Feed the Future' initiative and in 2013 during his eight day visit to Africa he launched 'Power Africa' initiative for bringing electricity to millions of households in the sub-Saharan Africa. A week before the summit on 28th July 2014, President Obama met 500 young African students under the 2014 Young African Leaders Initiative (YALI) launched in 2010 as a platform for giving opportunities to the next generation of Africa for excelling in various fields, kick starting pre-summit enthusiasm in Washington DC.[50]

Due to the immense success of the 1st US-Africa Leaders Summit, President Obama declared that the US- Africa Leaders Summit will henceforth be taken place every four years. In the coming time, the competition between the Americans and Chinese over the African resources is bound to escalate greatly, especially given the six out of ten fastest growing economies in the world are from Africa. The continent survived the economic crisis better than expected with growth in telecommunications, construction, transportation and banking. Nations have averaged growth rates of five to six percent the last decade. By 2050, one in four workers worldwide will be in Africa. It is clear that presently US lags far behind China in terms of forming great trade nexus and this summit is only a beginning to a possibly more flourishing US-Africa relations. Economically, China has managed to have an upper hand in the continent thanks to their business-like approach. But, even if US investments in Africa are unable to match the scope of their Chinese counterparts, what distinguishes the American presence in Africa is Washington's ability to assist on security matters. Though economic relations between US and Africa was the key highlight of the summit, matters like security, governance, human rights, women rights, climate change etc. was also highly discussed showcasing America's broader interest in the region.[51]

AU and Emerging Actors

The AU stated that China-Africa Cooperation Forum is a platform established by China and friendly African countries for collective consultation and dialogue and as a cooperation mechanism among developing countries. The characteristics of the Forum are twofold. First, it is to strengthen consultation and expand cooperation within a pragmatic framework and second, to promote political dialogue and economic cooperation with a view to seeking mutual reinforcement and cooperation. The Forum, which was established at Ministerial level, has held four sessions in Beijing, China, from 10-12 October 2000; in Addis Ababa, Ethiopia, from 15-16 December 2003; again in Beijing, from 4-5 November 2006; and in Sharm El Sheikh, Arab Republic of Egypt, on 8 November 2009. The 2006 session was at the level of Heads of State and Government to celebrate 60 years of diplomatic relations between Africa and China.

The FOCAC is a strong partnership, which has gestated over a long period of time. It is doing very well and has the potential of bringing various advantages to the two sides. In many areas, the partnership has delivered some concrete outcomes that are beneficial to Africa although Africa needs to utilize the partnership to the fullest in terms of the potential of the available market and the business opportunities. There is also need to align the partnership to the strategic objectives of the African Union. The magnificent new AU Conference and Office Complex built by the Chinese government free of charge to the AU and commissioned in January 2012, is testimony to the real value this partnership brings to Africa.

Of significance was the fact that the African Union Commission was admitted into FOCAC on 26 October 2011 as a full member and no more as an Observer, during the Senior Officials meeting held in Hahgzhou, China. It therefore attended the 5th Ministerial FOCAC meeting that took place in Beijing in 2012 in that capacity.[52]

China's presence in some of Africa's most conflict-ridden countries is well recognized. Under the banner of non-interference, Beijing has been able to finance resource investments, support Chinese-led infrastructure projects and encourage firms to open up businesses in countries that might otherwise be neglected because of sanctions or through the cautious approach adopted by most traditional donor countries and Western investors. As a result, China has been able to stake out a significant position in sectors and markets in countries as different as Angola, Ethiopia, Liberia, Sierra Leone, Chad, Sudan and South Sudan.[53]

However, these initial successes in achieving gains for both its own economic interests and that of the host government have been tempered in recent years by a series of significant setbacks rooted in that very state fragility that once seemed so accommodating. Renewed conflict in Sudan and South Sudan, for instance, has jeopardized China's attempts to protect its established economic interests and to expand new ones in the two states. Likewise, weak institutions and poor regulatory environments in Angola, Chad and Liberia have undermined Chinese business operations at various times, as has corruption and the arbitrary application of local laws. Moreover, some Chinese firms have themselves engaged in dubious practices in these fluid post-conflict settings, causing diplomatic incidents and reputational damage to the Chinese government's carefully crafted Africa policy.[54]

To date, the problems of African countries emerging out of conflict have not featured with any degree of dedicated significance in Chinese foreign policy towards the continent. This is despite the fact that Chinese investment and commodity-backed loans have played a notable and important role in the economies of post-conflict states, providing rapid outlay of finance and the construction of vital infrastructure at a time when other traditional sources of financing have been slow to respond. The result is that Chinese involvement in these states is both significant and highly visible and, as a consequence, particularly vulnerable to the problems that accompany state fragility, including weak administrative structures and the contested legitimacy of the host government. From South Sudan to the Democratic Republic of Congo, the pressures on Chinese actors embedded in the local environment have exerted commensurate demands on Beijing to respond effectively to address these difficult circumstances.[55]

The fallout of these inherently unstable conditions in Africa, however, extends beyond narrower Chinese economic concerns: China's position as a permanent UN Security Council member means continual exposure to the management challenges posed by threats to international peace and security that periodically arise from post-conflict states and, as such, China is expected to weigh in constructively to address these problems. Western Security Council members, Organization for Economic Cooperation and Development-Development Assistance Committee (OECD-DAC) donors, leading international financial institutions and non-government organizations all have established (if evolving) approaches towards post-conflict environments and fragile states. African governments and regional institutions give prominence to interventionist-oriented policies aimed at supporting the difficult transition from conflict to peaceful development.[56]

China notably lacks any such post-conflict and fragile state policy. Therefore, devising an approach towards post-conflict environments and fragile states has come to preoccupy Chinese policymakers and researchers working on African affairs in recent years. However, engaging with this complex topic has highlighted a number of difficult issues for China that render a simple adaptation to established approaches if not untenable, then certainly unpalatable. Coupled with a distinct ambivalence towards the interventionist character of Western-inspired "liberal peace" approaches, the absence of a post-conflict and fragile states policy sits uneasily with Beijing's commitment to play a greater activist role in international affairs generally and in support of African interests in particular. The result is a conscious effort to move away from ad hoc participation in African post-conflict settings to gradualist forms of engagement that include fomenting common Chinese–African values and re-imagining liberal norms on intervention. In short, China is in the process of becoming a norms maker in Africa.[57]

Similarly, Brazil's approach towards Africa emphasises long term partnership and mutual benefit in both political and economic spheres, under the banner of "South – South" cooperation. While political cooperation leads the way for this relationship, Brazil's rapidly rising business sector is already tapping the substantial opportunities offered by many of Africa's fast growing economies. 'Brazil-Africa Forum 2012' brought together leading figures from both Brazil and Africa, with keynote addresses, panel discussions and case studies addressing the strong cultural and socioeconomic similarities between the two regions.[58]

Brazil and Sub-Saharan Africa are re-establishing a robust engagement, after over 200 years. The two regions are natural partners with strong historic and cultural links and similar geological and climatic conditions. Because of these shared conditions, Brazilian technology is easily adapted to Africa. Brazil has emerged as one of the world's strongest economies and is playing an important role in redefining "the global south" in the changing world architecture. Africa is rapidly changing and Brazil has expressed growing interest in supporting and taking part in its development.

Brazil's economic growth, its success in narrowing social inequality and its development experience offer lessons for African countries. Countries in Sub-Saharan Africa have requested cooperation from Brazil in five key areas: tropical agriculture, tropical medicine, vocational training, energy and social protection. Brazil's trade with Sub-Saharan Africa increased between 2000 and 2010 from U$2 billion to U$12 billion; with expectations of continuous growth in the coming years. There are some obstacles that are being addressed like ease of transport (air and maritime) and telecommunications. South-South partnering will play a major role in global knowledge, trade and investments in the coming years. The World Bank has demonstrated interest for playing key role in supporting ongoing partnerships between Sub-Saharan Africa and Brazil and South-south relations as a whole. [59]

Thus African geo-strategic reality has gained traction under globalization and the AU has become a facilitating factor in the inter-relatiships between Africa and the extra-regional powers, including the dominant and emerging ones. The AU has placed on dominant and emerging actors and their engagements with the African continent.

Endnotes

1   Tim Murithi, "Briefing: The African Union At Ten: An Appraisal", *African Affairs*, 111(445), 2012, pp. 662–669

2   See the statement of the Africa Group at the 11th UN Congress on Crime Prevention and Criminal Justice, 18–25 April 2005; the statement of the Coordinator of the Africa Group to the Chemical Weapons Convention, April 2003; and the Africa Group position statement to the UN Climate Negotiations, August 1997. Controversially, in May 2004, the Africa Group submitted and successfully achieved the election of Sudan to the UN Commission on Human Rights, see Economic and Social Council, press release ECOSOC/ 6110.

3   African Union, 'The Common African Position on the Proposed Reform of the United Nations: the Ezulwini Consensus' (EXT/EX.CL/2 (VII), African Union, Addis Ababa, 7–8 March 2005).

4   Ibid., p. 9.

5   Ibid.

6   Ibid.

7   Tim Murithi, 2012, p. 667.

8   Ibid, Currently there is no systematic analysis of the history of the voting record of the Africa Group.

9   Rik Schreurs, 1993 'L'Eurafrique dans les Négociations du Traité de Rome, 1956-1957', in Daniel Bach (ed). *L'Europe-Afrique: Le Maillon Manquant* (thematic issue), in *Politique Africaine*, no 49, March: 92-93.

10 Walter Kennes, 2000, *Small Developing Countries and Global Markets*, Houndmills: Macmillan.

11 Anna Dickson, 2004 'The Unimportance of Trade Preferences', in Karin Arts and Anna Dickson (eds). *EU Development Co-operation: From Model to Symbol*, Manchester and New York: Manchester University Press & Palgrave, pp 42-59.

12 John Ravenhill, 1985 *Collective Clientelism: The Lomé Conventions and North-South Relations*, New York: Columbia University Press.

13 Daniel Bach, "The European Union and Africa: Trade Liberalisation, Constructive Disengagement, and the Securitisation of Europe's External Frontiers", *Africa Review*, 3 (1), 2011, p.35.

14 Ibid.

15 Ibid, , p. 36.

16 Ibid.

17 Stephen Halper, 2010, *The Beijing Consensus: How China's Authoritarian Model Will Dominate the Twenty-First Century*, Philadelphia (PA): Basic Books.

18 Bach, 2011, p. 44.

19 Ibid.

20 John Davis, (ed). 2007 *Africa and the War on Terrorism*, Aldershot: Ashgate; Isabelle Mandraud, 2010 'En Deux Ans, AQMI a Enlevé 20 Occidentaux au Sahel', *Le Monde (Paris)*, 23 September, p. 6.

21 Hassan Boubakri, 2004 *Transit Migrations between Tunisia, Libya and Sub-Saharan Africa: Study Based on Greater Tunis,* Strasbourg: Council of Europe, MG-RCONF., pp. 2-3.

22 Ibid, p. 4

23 Trauner, Florian and Imke Kruse. 2008 *EC Visa Facilitation and Re-Admission Agreements: Implementing a New EU Security Approach in the Neighbourhood* (Working Document, no 290, April), Brussels: Centre for European Policy Studies, p. 16.

24 Lorenzo Gabrielli, 2009 *Regional and Inter-Regional Governance of Migrations between Europe and Sub-Saharan Africa* (European Doctoral Colloquium, Heidelberg, 9-11 October), Heidelberg: South Asia Institute., p.5

25 Trauner & Kruse, 2008, p. 17; see EU, 2006, pp.5-9

26 Judy Dempsey, 2011 'Inconsistency Backfires on European Union in Africa', *International Herald Tribune*, 24 January (http://www.nytimes.com/2011/01/25/world/europe/25ihtletter25.html — accessed on 25 January 2011).

27 BBC News, 2 October 2001.

28 Daniel Bach, 2011, p. 40.

29 Ibid.

30 EU. 2005 *EU Non-Paper on EU-Africa Strategic Partnership* (Luxembourg Presidency of the Council of the EU, Working Document, 11 April), Brussels: EU Secretariat, General Affairs and External Relations Division (http://www.eu2005.lu/en/actualites/documents_travail/   2005/04/11/ue-afrique/   — accessed on 15 September 2010).

31 Ibid.

32 Daniel Bach, 2008 'The EU's Strategic Partnership with the African Union', in John Akokpari et al (eds). *The African Union and its Institutions*, Johannesburg and Cape Town: Fanele & Centre for Conflict Resolution, pp 355-371.

33 EU. 2008 *The Implementation of the Africa-EU Strategic Partnership: Guidelines for Joint Experts Groups* — endorsed by the Africa-EU Ministerial Troika, 20-21 November (http:// ec.europa.eu/development/icenter/repository/11eme-Troika-meeting-Guidelines-for-Jointexperts-Groups_en.pdf — accessed on 15 September 2010)., p.4.

34 Ibid.

35 V Tywuschik and A Sherriff. 2009 *Beyond Structures? Reflections on the Implementation of the Joint Africa-EU Strategy* (ECDPM Discussion Paper, no 87, February), p.9

36 EU. 2010 *Africa-EU 14th Troika Meeting* — Draft Option Paper, 23 April (http://www.consilium.   europa.eu/uedocs/cms_Data/docs/pressdata/en/er/114049.pdf — accessed on 15 September 2010).

37   Daniel Bach (2008), "European Union and China in Africa" in Kweku Ampiah & Sanua Naidu, eds., *Crouching Tiger, Hidden Dragon? China in Africa: Engaging the World's next superpower*, University of Kwazulu Natal Press.

38   Ibid.

39   Ibid.

40   Ibid.

41   Ibid.

42   Ibid.

43   Ibid.

44   Ibid.

45   AU-USA, http://www.au.int/en/partnerships/au_usa

46   Stephanie Hanson (2009), "The African Union" http://www.cfr.org/africa-sub-saharan/african-union/p11616

47   Ibid.

48   Aakriti Sethi, "Backgrounder, 1st US-Africa Leaders Summit: A New Chapter in the US-Africa Relations", August 20, 2014 http://www.idsa.in/backgrounder/1s tUSAfricaLeadersSummit_AakritiSethi_200814.html

49   Ibid.

50   Ibid.

51   Ibid.

52   AU, Africa – China, http://www.au.int/en/partnerships/africa_china

53   Chris Alden and Daniel Large, "On Becoming a Norms Maker: Chinese Foreign Policy, Norms Evolution and the Challenges of Security in Africa", *The China Quarterly*, 2015, p.1.

54   Ibid, p. 2.

55   Ibid.

56   Ibid.

57   Ibid, p. 3.

58   Karin Costa Vazquez (2012), "Brazil-Africa Forum: Building New Partnerships for the 21st Century", http://www.southsouth.info/profiles/blogs/brazil-africa-forum-building-new-partnerships-for-the-21st

59   World Bank, "Brazil and Sub-Saharan Africa: South-South Partnering for Growthhttp://web.worldbank.org/WBSITE/EXTERNAL/COUNTRIES/AFRICAEXT/0,,contentMDK:23061951~pagePK:146736~piPK:226340~theSitePK:258644,00.html

Chapter - 6

AU-India Engagement: A Comprehensive Perspective

India has developed a three-layered cooperation with Africa through the traditional bilateral engagement with African states and multilateral engagement at the continental level through the African Union (AU), and at the regional level, India has engaged Regional Economic Communities (RECs). As a development partner, India has recognised the importance attached by the African leaderships to the process of regional integration. India and Africa relations have reached a decisive stage with the commencement of first India Africa Forum Summit (IAFS-I) in the year 2008. The historic IAFS process has not only provided an institutional framework of cooperation at three levels (continental, regional and bilateral), but also has instilled a new momentum to the relations in a comprehensive scale.

In the two India-Africa Forum Summits held so far, four joint policy documents were pronounced. The Delhi Declaration and India-Africa Framework for Cooperation adopted in IAFS-I in the year 2008 defined the future roadmap for cooperation between India and African countries. The Addis Ababa Declaration and the Africa India Framework for Enhanced Cooperation adopted at the IAFS-II in the year 2011 guided a systematic and enhanced engagement between India and Africa. The Addis Ababa Declaration is a political document covering issues of bilateral, regional and international interest to India and Africa, including the common position on UN reforms, WTO, international terrorism, etc. The Africa India Framework for Enhanced Cooperation spells out the agreed areas of cooperation.

This chapter has contextualized the growing engagement between AU and India under wider canvas of AU's interface with the extra-regional powers.

It has analysed the trends of AU-India relationships in security, political and economic levels. It has explored the scope for policy calibration in this three-levelled relationship.

India-AU Political Relations

India is a member of the AU Partners Group (AUPG), which meets periodically in Addis Ababa. Since its inception of the AU, India has been regularly participating in its various Summits. Dr. Shashi Tharoor, MoS for External Affairs, participated in the 14th Ordinary Summit of The African Union from 25th January to 2nd February, 2010, whose theme was "Information and Communication Technologies in Africa: Prospects and Challenges for Development". He attended the opening ceremony of the Executive Council, called on the Ethiopian Prime Minister, Foreign Ministers of a number of African states and Mr. Jean Ping, Chairperson of AUC and discussed a number of matters of mutual interest. During the visit, he also inaugurated the Tele-medicine facility at the African Union Clinic which received wide publicity.[1]

Vivek Katju, Secretary(West) participated in the Ministerial segment of the 15th Ordinary Summit of the African Union Commission which took place in Kampala from July 21-24, 2010. Preneet Kaur, MOS (PK), visited Addis Ababa and participated in the Ministerial segment of the 16th Ordinary Summit of the African Union which was held in Addis Ababa between January 26-28, 2011. During her stay, she addressed the 18th Ordinary Session of the Executive Council of the African Union, on January 27, 2011. MOS(PK) met Chairperson of the African Union Commission, Dr. Jean Ping and also held bilateral meetings with many Ministers from African countries such as South Africa, Swaziland, Mauritania, Mauritius, and Executive Secretary of IGAD. She also called on the Deputy Prime Minister and Foreign Minister of Ethiopia. M. Ganapathi, Secretary (West) attended the 19th Ordinary Session of the Executive Council in January 2012.[2]

Indian Vice President Mohammad Hamid Ansari represented New Delhi at the 50th Anniversary Summit of OAU/AU held in Addis Ababa on May 25, 2013. He delivered his address:

The establishment of the OAU this day 50 years ago was an event of global significance. The African Union must take a large part of the credit for the emancipation of the African people from colonialism and apartheid. Over the past five decades, Africa has stood tall, its vision firmly focused on the future of its youth, inspired by the wide horizons and the beauty of its land and drawing from the wellsprings of wisdom of its ancients. Pan Africanism as an ideology inspired the founding fathers of Africa. The African Union today is the modulated, considered voice of Africa, committed to the vision of peace, progress and prosperity for its myriad peoples. Our own founding fathers believed that India's freedom would remain incomplete as long as Africa remained in bondage. History records that India imposed a trade embargo on apartheid South Africa in 1946 and took the lead in placing apartheid on the agenda of the very first session of the United Nations General Assembly. Our partnership with Africa is anchored in the fundamental principles of equality, mutual respect and mutual benefit that should, we hope, serve to redefine the contours of the international order on more egalitarian lines. Our development partnership with Africa has been illuminated by this experience. Reinvigorated and multi-dimensional in scope, the India-Africa partnership is today being taken forward under the India-Africa Forum Summit process. Anchored in the philosophy of South South cooperation, our approach is non intrusive and non prescriptive, consultative and, above all, responsive to Africa's own assessments of its needs.[3]

Dr. Alpha Oumar Konare, Chairperson of AU Commission paid an official visit to India from 19-21 December 2006. He called on the President, had meetings with the EAM, MOS (AS), and delivered a lecture at the Indian Council of World Affairs (ICWA). He also visited TCIL and IGNOU and observed the working of the Pan African tele-education project.

Commissioner for Political Affairs and Commissioner for Infrastructure & Energy participated in the Federalism Conference and India- Africa Hydrocarbon Conference respectively in Nov. 2007. Commissioner for Rural Economy & Agriculture participated in Avian Influenza Conference in December 2007. Commissioner for Economic Affairs of AU participated in the Partnership Summit 2008 in March 2008 and spoke on "Ensuring Growth, Making it Inclusive: The West Asian and African Views." Deputy Chairperson of AUC, Commissioner for Trade and Industry and Commissioner for Infrastructure & Energy participated in the India Africa Forum Summit in April 2008. Commissioner for Infrastructure attended Exim Bank Conclave in Delhi in March, 2009. The Commissioner for Human

Resources and Science and Technology visited India in September 2010 and held discussions with Secretary (West) and Secretary, DARE and DG, ICAR. He also interacted with FICCI, National University for Educational Planning and Administration and visited TCIL. He is again visiting India as leader of AU delegation for the S&T Ministerial Conference taking place in New Delhi on March 1 & 2, 2012.[4]

India-Africa Forum Summit

The first ever India-Africa Forum Summit, attended by the countries representing AU and the Regional Economic Communities of Africa, was held in New Delhi on 8-9 April, 2008. Leaders of 14 African countries and the African Union Commission participated. It represented a turning point in the India-AU relations. The Summit adopted the Delhi Declaration and the Africa-India Framework for Cooperation, which constituted the blueprint for cooperation between India and Africa in the 21st century. India announced unilateral duty free and preferential market access for exports from all Least Developed Countries, 34 of which are in Africa. The scheme covers 94% of India's total tariff lines with preferential market access on tariff lines that comprise 92.55 of global exports of all Least Developed Countries. Products of immediate interest to Africa include cotton, cocoa, aluminium ores, copper ores, cashew nuts, cane sugar, ready-made garments, fish fillets and non-industrial diamonds. India was to double its quantum of credit to USD 5.4 billion from the present USD 2.15 billion over next five years.[5]

In order to enhance opportunities for African Students to pursue higher studies in India, the Government of India doubled long-term scholarships for undergraduates, postgraduates and higher courses and increased the number of training slots under our technical assistance programmes from 1100 to 1600 every year. Prime Minister also proposed to enhance Indian aid to Africa by expanded concessional lines of credit and undertaking projects against grants in excess of USD 500 million over the next five to six years, focusing on human resource development and capacity building. India will strengthen local capabilities by creating regional and pan –African institutions of higher education, especially in pure sciences, information technology and vocational education. India also committed to make investments in research and development in renewable forms of energy and agricultural development, through these institutions.

Several outreach events took place before or concurrent with the Summit. These were (i) the first ever India-Africa Editors Conference;(ii) joint performances by Indian and African cultural troupes; (iii) a seminar of intellectuals from Africa and India on India-Africa Partnership on the 21st century(vi) a programme for youth and women from Africa; and (v) a business conclave.

Following visit of a high level delegation from AUC to New Delhi, a Joint Action Plan, with a view to implementing the decisions of the IAFS 2008, was launched on 10th March 2010 between the Government of India and the African Union. More than 40 scholars have already joined Indian universities subsequent to the award 300 Ph.D and masters scholarships in the field of Agriculture over a period of four years. Under the CV Raman International Fellowship for African Researchers, 85 African researchers have already been availed of the scholarship last year and for the second edition applications have already reached FICCI. These are short-term, fully-funded scholarships. FICCI has been designated as the coordinating partner for this fellowship programme. Under capacity building initiatives various short-term courses were organised for some 432 African experts on subjects such as economic offences and cyber crimes, food quality and safety, disaster risk management, infrastructure development, entrepreneur development, combating desertification and the like. (62 of the 432 have been from Ethiopia). After the decisions taken during the AIFS-II, new courses have already begun.

The Second Africa-India Forum Summit took place in Addis Ababa from May 20-25, 2011. The AIFS-II, saw the first ever State visit of the Prime Minister of India to Ethiopia. The PM inaugurated the IAFS-II in Addis Ababa in on 24-25 May 2011, which was attended, in addition to India and the African Union Commission, by HOSs/HOGs of 15 African Countries or their representatives. The Prime Minister announced a new credit line of US $ 300 million for Djibouti-Ethiopia Railway line as regional integration component of the decisions taken under the Summits. Two documents, namely 1. the Framework for enhanced cooperation and 2. The Addis Ababa Declaration were adopted during the summit. The PM hosted a lunch over the Retreat at the Sheraton Hotel. On 25th May 2011, the Summit concluded with the release of a book namely "A Billion Dreams", a commemorative stamp and a special edition of the Africa Quarterly. On the 24th May 2011 the PM held a series of bilateral meetings with various African leaders and the

AU Chairperson, Dr. Jean Ping. The Ethiopian PM and Chairperson of the AUC, Dr. Jean Ping called on PM on May 23, 2011 at the Sheraton hotel.[6]

Minister of Commerce and Industry, Mr. Anand Sharma inaugurated India Africa Trade Ministers meet on May 21, 2011. Trade Ministers from 17 African Countries participated. A Joint statement was issued at the end of the Trade Ministers' meet. The Trade Ministers also met a group of Indian and African CEOs and the Minister of Commerce and industry held a press conference after the meet. This event has been announced to be a regular one in the future It has also been decided to establish an India Africa Business Council for which preparations have already begun with the Indian side having decided on the co-chair and membership. The African side has also submitted names of 27 members. The name of the co-chair from the African side is expected soon.

Apart from these major high level visits, there were a series of side events organized alongside the AIFS-II. The first ever Academic symposium captioned ""Africa & India : Partnership for Enhancing Development & Growth" was organized from 11-12 May 2011, which saw a participation of academicians from different parts of Africa and adoption of a document which was presented at the ministerial level meeting at the AUC on 24th May 2011. The cultural show named "Rhythm of Life" was inaugurated by the First Lady H.E. Mrs. Azeb Mesfin and the Commerce and Industry Minister Shri Anand Sharma from 20-22 May 2011. The cultural show saw the fusion of some of the African dance and music with the Indian dance and music and was well appreciated. A multi-media exhibition held from May 20-22, 2011 and named "From Tradition to Innovation" was also inaugurated by Shri Anand Sharma and the First Lady H.E. Mrs. Azeb Mesfin on May 20, 2011.

The Trade Exhibition called "India Show" was inaugurated by Shri Anand Sharma and his Ethiopian counterpart Mr. Abdurhman Sheikh Mohammed, Minister for Trade and Mr. Mekonnen Manyazewal Minister for Industry and the Mr. Tadesse Haile State Minister for Industry, and the African Union Commission Deputy Chairperson, Mr. Erastus Mwencha from 20 – 22 May 2011. A "Handcrafting Hope" exhibition, also held between 20–22 May 2011 saw the participation of some of the African craftswomen and their Indian counterparts who displayed some of the common features amongst them. A Film Festival captioned "Come, Fall in Love with the Magic of Bollywood" show was inaugurated during the same time by the Culture Minister of Ethiopia and Secretary (West) and AU Commissioner for Social affairs, and saw a huge turnout of people for viewing the films from 20 – 27 May, 2011. The India Africa Media Partnership Symposium called "Building Bridges" was held on 21 May 2011. From the African Union, AU commissioner for Rural economy and Agriculture Ms. Tumusime Rhoda Peace attended the inauguration.

The Trade Exhibition called "India Show" was inaugurated by Shri Anand Sharma and his Ethiopian counterpart Mr. Abdurhman Sheikh Mohammed, Minister for Trade and Mr. Mekonnen Manyazewal Minister for Industry and the Mr. Tadesse Haile State Minister for Industry, and the African Union Commission Deputy Chairperson, Mr. Erastus Mwencha from 20 – 22 May 2011. A "Handcrafting Hope" exhibition, also held between 20–22 May 2011 saw the participation of some of the African craftswomen and their Indian counterparts who displayed some of the common features amongst them. A Film Festival captioned "Come, Fall in Love with the Magic of Bollywood" show was inaugurated during the same time by the Culture Minister of Ethiopia and Secretary (West) and AU Commissioner for Social affairs, and saw a huge turnout of people for viewing the films from 20 – 27 May, 2011. The India Africa Media Partnership Symposium called "Building Bridges" was held on 21 May 2011. From the African Union, AU commissioner for Rural economy and Agriculture Ms. Tumusime Rhoda Peace attended the inauguration.[7]

India and African Union Commission are in the process of discussing a Joint Plan of Action subsequent to the AIFS-II. In this regard, the first meeting took place in Addis Ababa in October 2011, when Shri Gurjit Singh, AS (E&SA) visited and led the Indian delegation. The process of discussions is currently on. During the just concluded AU Summit in January 2012, further discussions took place between the Indian delegation led by AS (E&SA) and the AU wherein AU was requested to submit their response by end-February so that the Plan of Action could be signed as soon as possible. AU was also requested to convey the names of 6 institutions to be set up at continental level.[8]

Pan-African e-Network Project

The proposal for establishing the Pan-African e-Network Project was made by the then President of India at the Pan-African Parliament in 2004 and is being implemented in conjunction with the African Union.

The Project was inaugurated by Shri Pranab Mukherjee, the then Minister of External Affairs on February 26, 2009 from the TCIL Centre in New Delhi. The process to implement the project was undertaken by establishing a Steering Committee, which is co-chaired by the Commissioner for Infrastructure and the India's Permanent Representative to the African Union (the Indian Ambassador to Ethiopia). An agreement between GOI and the African Union was signed in New Delhi in October 2005 and seven meetings of the Steering Committee have so far been held. The meetings are co-chaired by the Ambassador of India, who is also the Permanent Representative of India to AU, with the Commissioner for Infrastructure Development of AU. JS (WA) and representatives from IGNOU, TCIL, and Amity University also participate in the deliberations. The 7th Meeting of the Steering Committee took place in May 2010.

Ethiopia was the first beneficiary of the project under a pilot project, which was completed in 2009 at a cost of US$2.13 million.[9] India has also committed to provide tele-medicine, tele-education and VVIP connectivity facility at AU Commission in Addis Ababa. A tele-medicine Centre was inaugurated by the then MOS (ST), Dr Shashi Tharoor on February 28, 2010 during his visit to Addis Ababa in connection with the 14th Summit of AU. AU thus became the 48th member of the Network. Pan-African E-network project was inaugurated in February 2009 by the then External Affairs Minister of India. Another inauguration took place on August 16, 2010 when Shri S.M. Krishna, External Affairs Minister of India interacted live with 12 Ministers of African countries. 23 countries have been covered by this network where the project has been fully implemented.

India had allocated 13 slots each in the years 2008-2010 under the Indian Technical and Economic Cooperation (ITEC) Programme to the AU Commission personnel and all the slots were been fully utilized. After the AIFS-II, the slots have been increased to 30.[10]

India-AU Security Cooperation

Among the various aspects of engagement with the African Union Commission, their requirement for training and capacity building of their nascent standby brigade, which were to be the building blocks of their peacekeeping activities, are being discussed. At the request of the AU commission, initial discussions on their structures to be developed and capabilities to be enhanced were undertaken between an Indian military delegation and the peace and security division of the AU Commission in August 2006. The aim was to see how the Indian experience can be shared with the AU's efforts to enhance its own capacities for peacekeeping operations in Africa.[11]

India and Africa continue their close security cooperation, including through regular consultations at the UN, at the AU and in New Delhi/national capitals. New Delhi has defence cooperation with several African countries, including South Africa, Mauritius, Seychelles, Kenya, Tanzania, Mozambique and Nigeria. India has signed its first strategic partnership with South Africa. Both remain committed towards operationalisation of the African Standby Force through special training programmes. This cooperation has been appreciated in the UN, in the AU, in the regional entities like ECOWAS of India's contribution in peacekeeping, in providing security in the countries which are in the conflict zone in Africa.

India's contribution to the United Nations Peacekeeping Operations (UNPKO) is acknowledged globally, especially in Africa. India has become part of the conflict-containment and reconstruction process of the affected region. As the third largest contributor of personnel to the UNPKO, India's significant participation in the conflict-containment and reconstruction process is recognized in Africa. India has more than 5,000 peacekeepers in Africa. In 2007, India's unparalleled contribution of a 125-member Female Formed Police Unit (FFPU) of its paramilitary Central Reserve Police Force (CRPF) to the UN Mission in Liberia represents the first-ever women contingent in the history of UN peacekeeping. The Indian women police force deployment has emerged as a source of inspiration for the conflict-affected women in Liberia and wider West Africa.

In the context of issues relating to international peace and security, India has appreciated efforts made by the AUPSC in maintaining peace in Africa. New Delhi recognizes the role of African countries in maintaining peace and security in the continent and their participation in peacekeeping missions in other parts of the world. India is supportive of the ongoing effort of developing an African Standby Force for enhancing the continent's capacity to maintain peace and security. Africa, on its part, also appreciates India's principled support to and continuing involvement with UN peacekeeping operations, especially in the African continent. Moreover, India has engaged with Africa as one of its crucial partners in the electoral process. New Delhi has approved US$ 10 million to the UN fund, and has promised an additional amount of US$ 2 million for the purchase of protective gear, to combat the Ebola epidemic.

India's security cooperation with Africa needs a greater thrust. As a victim of terrorism, India could partner in the proposed multilateral and regional counter-terror initiatives in Africa. Moreover, India's position in the case of politico-armed intra-state conflicts in Africa – i.e. protection of the sovereignty and territorial integrity of the conflict afflicted country along with the sensitivity towards the legitimate aspirations of its people - needs to be articulated in a more proactive and pronounced fashion. While this policy articulation has to be undertaken through bilateral channel, at the AU and regional levels, logistical, personnel and capacity building support have to be provided.

India's Partnership with African RECs

New Delhi thrust particular focus on the African RECs in its current engagement with the continent. Africa has more than 40 RECs and the AU has recognised eight of them. These major RECs include Economic Community of Central African States (ECCAS), Inter-Governmental Authority for Development (IGAD), East African Community (EAC), Economic Community of West African States (ECOWAS), Common Market for Eastern and Southern Africa (COMESA), Southern African Development Community (SADC), Community of Sahelo-Saharan States (CEN-SAD) and Arab Maghreb Union (UMA).[12]

Over the decades, these groupings have moved towards harmonisation of standards and rules as well as creation of common markets. These multilateral institutions have been working towards better movement of goods and services through enhanced infrastructure development and regional integration, along with the development of processing facilities, particularly in agriculture, mining and oil and gas. This process of regional integration has an important bearing on the development of India's trade and investment relations with the African countries. The African RECs have demonstrated eagerness to engage with India's private sector to attract them for greater trade and investment opportunities. These RECs have also expressed their desire to sensitise Indian agencies on Africa's requirements in the field of capacity building, human resource development, food processing and agriculture.[13]

The eight RECs, recognised by the AU, constitute an integral part of the India Africa Forum Summit (IAFS) structure, based on the decision taken at the AU Summit held in Gambian capital Banjul in July 2006. As per the Banjul Formula, the countries chairing these eight RECs were invited to the first IAFS held in New Delhi in April 2008. The three-layered engagement between India and Africa, including cooperation at regional level, was recognised under the IAFS process. The Action Plan of the 1st IAFS had certain components of development support allocated at the regional level. The Action Plan for the 2nd IAFS, launched on September 6, 2013, had several regional initiatives as well. India has proposed to establish 32 regional institutions, the locations of which have been decided in consultation with the RECs. Furthermore, New Delhi has supported the AU's efforts at promoting regional integration by extending a Line of Credit (LOC) worth US$ 300 million for Ethiopia-Djibouti railway line.[14]

As part of India's attempt to reinvigorate its linkage with the African RECs, New Delhi has so far signed Memorandum of Understanding (MoUs) with EAC, COMESA, ECOWAS, SADC and IGAD under which discussions take place at official/ministerial levels. There has been a proposal for signing MoU with the ECCAS as well. New Delhi's engagement with these RECs becomes all the more significant, since there is a recent trend towards inter-regional connectivity across the Africa economic space. For instance, a free trade zone in eastern and southern Africa is likely to be completed in 2015. The Tripartite Free Trade Agreement, being negotiated among the SADC, COMESA, and EAC representatives, is estimated to benefit 600 million people living in 26 African countries, or half of the AU member countries, with a combined domestic product of about US$ 1 trillion.[15]

India's linkages with the regional groupings in Africa reached a decisive stage with the commencement of 1st India-RECs Meeting in New Delhi on November 14-16, 2010. While India had earlier engaged with some of the African RECs and had signed MoU with four of them, but on this occasion an initiative was taken to engage all of them together at one platform. Such institutionalised engagement has provided greater space for deliberations on the implementation of the India Africa Action Plan for the Framework of Cooperation and working out implementation procedures. The first India-African RECs Meeting was attended by the Secretary Generals of COMESA and EAC, the President of the ECOWAS, the Deputy Executive Secretary of

SADC, Adviser in-charge of Political Affairs of CEN-SAD, the Director of Political Affairs of UMA and the senior officials.[16]

The 2nd India-African RECs Meeting was organised in New Delhi on November 8-9, 2011. The meeting was attended by the Secretaries General of COMESA, EAC, and ECCAS, the Executive Secretary of IGAD and representatives from the SADC and the ECOWAS along with the senior officials from their delegations. The representatives of the RECs met with several Departments/Ministries/Agencies of the Indian Government engaged in implementing jointly agreed programme and projects. The delegations from the RECs visited Indian Agricultural Research Institute, Pusa and also participated in an academic interaction organised by the Indian Council of World Affairs (ICWA), Sapru House. On 8 November 2011, a MoU on Economic Cooperation was signed between India and the IGAD. It was agreed that the periodic dialogue with the RECs would continue and appropriate action plans, including all decisions taken through the Joint Action Plan with the AU, would be pursued together.[17]

The 3rd India-African RECs Meeting was held in New Delhi on August 20-21, 2014. The meeting was attended by the Secretary General of EAC, Executive Secretary of IGAD, Acting Secretary General of CEN-SAD, Assistant Secretary General of COMESA and Director of ECCAS. The RECs delegations called on India's Minister of State for External Affairs, General Dr. V.K. Singh (Retd.) on August 20, 2014. They interacted with several Departments/Ministries/Agencies of the Government of India along with some civil society organizations, business association, educational institutions and think tanks, such as Department of Agriculture Research and Educations, Barefoot College, Tilonia, The Energy and Resources Institute, Confederation of Indian Industry, Telecommunications Consultants India Ltd. The representatives of the RECs also participated in an academic interaction organised by the ICWA, Sapru House. This meeting has an immense significance, since India is going to host the crucial 3rd IAFS in the year 2015.[18]

India-African RECs Meeting processes have provided inputs into New Delhi's Africa policy and also streamlined initiatives in the form of training, financial assistance and LOCs. More importantly, it has projected that India is keen on taking feedback from different stakeholders and tailoring its initiatives as per their priorities and preferences. This has created an Indo-African synergy in political, economic and related domains. The attempts must be made to deepen the partnership in the infrastructure and capacity building projects, which would foster intra- and inter-regional economic connectivity in Africa.[19]

Thus, India has developed a three-layered cooperation with Africa through the traditional bilateral engagement with African states and multilateral engagement at the continental level through the AU, and at the regional level, India has engaged African RECs. The growing engagement between the AU and India, which has steadily gained substance on political, security and economic fronts, has captured immense significance under wider canvas of AU's interface with the extra-regional powers.

Scale of India-Africa Electioneering Partnership

India has cultivated mutuality of interests and world views through century-long engagements with Africa. Over sixty year long experiment of democracy with the world's largest, yet substantially poor and diverse, electorate has enabled India to claim its democratic experience unique. Africa, with its historic subjugation and current resurgence, supports India's claim by engaging with it as one of the crucial partners on the issue of political development. The partnership on electioneering has steadily become a critical component of India-Africa collaborative efforts of building 'procedural' democracy in their regions.

Reflecting on India's unique democratic experiment, Ashutosh Varshney argues that universal suffrage came to most Western democracies only after the Industrial Revolution, which meant that the poor got the right to vote only after those societies had become relatively rich; a welfare state has attended to the needs of low-income segments of the population; and the educated and the wealthy have tended to vote more than the poor. He describes Indian experience as different on all three counts: India adopted universal suffrage at the time of independence, long before the transition to a modern industrialized economy began; the country does not have an extensive welfare system, although it has made a greater effort to create one of late; and, defying democratic theory, a great participatory upsurge has marked Indian politics.[20]

Similar spirits and patterns of democratic experiment against 'standard' structural constrains have also been evident in today's Africa. Nevertheless, African political development trajectory has got its own share of uniqueness in terms of taking shape under the active support of the regional groupings under the leadership of the AU, which is having a strong Pan-African undertone and anti-colonial embeddedness. A trend towards civilian led electoral governance systems, with 'limited yet sometimes frequent' military interregnum, has indeed gained traction across the African continent through the constant institutional interventions and protections of the AU led regional actors.

Based on the common colonial experience, political development partnership between India and Africa remains an invariable basis of their strong relations. While India is trying to move from a 'procedural' to a 'substantive' democratic process, all most all African countries are engaged in a strong quest for their democratic entitlements. Electoral politics remains a critical, though not the exhaustive, aspect of the issue of democratic governance. As historic partners of political development, India and Africa have engaged in the cooperation on electioneering process over the decades.

Before going into greater detail India-Africa direct engagement, it is pertinent to briefly mention their recent cooperation on the electoral management through global multilateral platforms such as United Nations Development Programme (UNDP) and Commonwealth Observers Group. As part of ongoing UNDP project, a seven-member delegation from the Electoral Commission of Namibia (ECN) visited Bangalore city in southern Indian province of Karnataka in April 2014 to witness election management. ECN team saw live webcasting of the polls undertaken with the assistance of college students and volunteers. The team also interacted with the transgender voters of the Hebbal Dasarahalli area in the Bangalore North parliamentary constituency. Namibia has purchased 1,700 EVMs and ordered 3,400 more from Indian manufacturer Bharat Electronics Limited.[21] Similarly in as recent as October 2014, the former Chief Election Commissioner (CEC) of India Dr. S. Y. Quraishi observed the elections in Mozambique as a member of the Commonwealth Observers Group.

The UNDP and Election Commission of India (ECI) have signed a Memorandum of Understanding (MoU) in 2012 to promote the exchange of knowledge and experience in the field of election management. The purpose of this MOU is to provide a framework of cooperation and facilitate collaboration between ECI and UNDP to promote South-South Collaboration, on mutually agreed terms and conditions in the mutually identified priority areas in the field of electoral management and administration, including: a) promoting the exchange of knowledge, experience and expertise in the field of electoral management and administration; b) assisting in the identification of capacity ends with a focus on strengthening electoral systems and democratic institutions and designing learning and exchange programmes; c) facilitate relationships with other electoral authorities and organizations; and d) any other modality of cooperation as mutually agreed by the parties. [22]

In order to operationalize activities in the areas of cooperation outlined in the MoU, UNDP is implementing a project on "Supporting Democratic Electoral Management" for the cycle 2013-17 with the broad outcome of "Promoting the exchange of knowledge and experiences in the field of election management and administration through ECI to other developing countries." One of the other focus areas in the UNDP-ECI project is to make elections more inclusive and increase voter education. [23]

Coming to the direct engagement between India and Africa on the electoral cooperation, the first Sudanese parliamentary elections were conducted by Sukumar Sen, the then CEC of India in as early as 1953. Formed in 1957, the Sudanese Election Commission drew on Indian elections laws. [24] In the recent joint policy documents, including the significant *Africa-India Framework for Enhanced Cooperation* declared under the India Africa Forum Summit (IAFS)-II in 2011, India and Africa recognize the importance of democratic governance, human rights, decentralization, justice system, institutions of parliamentary democracy and election. They agree to enhance cooperation by sharing of experiences and capacity building, where necessary, among election commissions, the institutions of parliamentary democracy and media organizations. [25]

Subsequent to summit level policy articulation of their commitment to partner on such political issues, India has signed MoU with some African countries in the field of electoral management and administration. India and Egypt signed MoU on Cooperation in the field of electoral management and administration in the year 2012. [26] In November 2012 a four-member delegation, led by the Deputy Chairman of the High National Election Commission of Libya, visited India and an MOU was signed between the two election commissions. [27] India and Mauritius signed MoU on Cooperation in election management and administration in the year 2013. [28] Indian External Affairs Minister (EAM) Salman Khurshid paid a two-day official visit to Tunisia in February 2014 in a first ever bilateral visit at EAM level from India since the establishment of diplomatic relations between the two countries in 1958. He informed the Tunisian leadership of India's readiness to share its expertise in building durable institutions of democracy, particularly in connection with voting methods and the work of the election commission.[29]

ECI's capacity building collaboration with its counter parts of African countries on electoral management have gained momentum with establishment of India International Institute of Democracy and Election Management (IIDEM) in the year 2011. The first phase of IIDEM was jointly inaugurated at the ECI premises in New Delhi by the then CEC of India Dr. S. Y. Quraishi and Election Commissioner from Kenya Ken Nyaundi. The delegates from South Africa and Commonwealth Secretariat were part of the inauguration function. The first course of IIDEM was held for the Electoral Commission of Kenya in June 2011.

Furthermore, a nine-member delegation from the Independent National Electoral Commission of Nigeria had a study visit to the IIDEM in September 2011. The delegation was headed by Prof. Lai Olurode, National Commissioner and comprised three other National Commissioners, namely Ambassador Ahmed Wali, Dr. Abdulkadir S. Oniyangi, Engr. (Dr.) Nuru Yakubu, and Barr. Kassim Gana Gaidam-Resident Electoral Commissioner. They were accompanied by four senior officials.[30] Again another 14-member Senate Committee of Senators & Members of House of Representatives of Nigerian Parliament at the invitation of CEC visited India in June 2014 and was hosted by ECI.[31]

IIDEM is established by the ECI as an advanced resource centre of learning, research, training and extension for participatory democracy and election management. The institute aims at becoming a national and international hub for exchange of good practices in election management. IIDEM's objective is to direct its efforts to enhance the potential and capacity of the election commission and its officials in carrying out their mandate and functions in a more effective and professional manner. It carries the goal of meticulous, accurate, voter friendly implementation of election processes by committed, competent, credible and skilled managers and associated groups. It intends to work for promoting democratic values and practices, enhancing voter education and awareness and developing human resource and capacities for efficient conduct of free and fair elections in India and for developing mutually beneficial partnership as well as collaborations with other countries.[32]

IDEM has four components. These are: a) training and capacity development, b) voter education and civic participation, c) research, innovation and documentation and d) international projects and technical collaboration. The institute is being developed in collaboration with the Indian Government, United Nations, the Commonwealth and inter-governmental organisations like Sweden based International Institute of Democracy and Electoral Assistance (IDEA). The 54 member Commonwealth group has proposed to set up a resource centre for its member nations at IIDEM.[33] This creates greater scope for capacity building interaction between ECI and its Anglophone African counter parts. Commenting on the recently held election in Mozambique in October 2014 after being directly part of it as a Commonwealth Observer, Dr. S. Y. Quraishi estimated that so far around 40 countries across the world have sent election management officials to IIDEM. He also suggested for Mozambican election management officials to be part of IIDEM's international interaction exercise.[34]

Exploring Scope for India-AU Electoral Partnership

India is a member of the AU Partners Group. New Delhi has elevated its relationship with Africa to the summit level and has developed an institutional framework for a three-layered cooperation. The AU has consequently become the continental representative of this engagement, which has taken a comprehensive shape under the India Africa Forum Summit (IAFS) process. Delivering his address at the 50th Anniversary Summit of OAU/AU held in Addis Ababa on May 25, 2013, Indian Vice President Mohammad Hamid Ansari proclaimed, "The African Union today is the modulated, considered voice of Africa, committed to the vision of peace, progress and prosperity for its myriad peoples." He also noted, "Reinvigorated and multi-dimensional in scope, the India-Africa partnership is today being taken forward under the India-Africa Forum Summit process."[35]

The capacity building approach, which is inherent in the India-Africa engagement adding substance to the larger South-South cooperation agenda, has acquired greater significance and wider attention in the IAFS process. A number of skill development measures, including providing scholarships and building and strengthening institutions, have been taken up with renewed vigour at bilateral, regional and continental levels. As mentioned earlier, IAFS joint documents have referred to policy commitment for election management collaboration. There is, however, scope for further improvisation in electoral capacity building area in India-Africa cooperation at the AU level.

The interaction and exchange of experience can be initiated between India International Institute of Democracy and Election Management (IIDEM) of the Election Commission of India (ECI) and the Democracy and Electoral Assistance Unit (DEAU) in the Department of Political Affairs (DPA) of the African Union Commission (AUC). It is a matter of policy recognition that these two election management institutions have been respectively set up by the Government of India and the AU in coincidence with the IAFS time frame. The direct engagement between IIDEM and DEAU will increase the interaction between ECI officials and their African counter parts. This exchange programme so far tends to confine with Anglophone African countries, due to the MoU between IIDEM and Commonwealth group.

There is a commitment for India's support for endeavour towards Africa Standby Force and the African Court of Justice in IAFS policy documents. Since many conflict containment and conflict adjudication efforts have electoral dimension, IIDEM and ECI's further collaboration with the AU has greater scope in building electoral dispute settlement capacity. There has been steady functional interface between ECI and justice system in India on election issues. Thus, institutional interface between India and AU on election management exercise has the potential to address such common election management issues and contribute in strengthening 'procedural' democracy in India and Africa.

The media collaboration is a related area of cooperation between India and the AU. This has the capacity to form a positive global public opinion about elections across Africa and AU's constructing through authentic and balanced reporting on the issue. There is an increasing concern about the strategic use of political dissent of the African countries by the extra-regional actors, notably the Western power. Thus, India-AU media cooperation on electoral affairs can contribute to the ongoing efforts of forming synergy between African Peace and Security Architecture (APSA) and African Governance Architecture (AGA). Capacity building cooperation on 'procedural' democracy, therefore, remains an exclusively priority domain for enhancing partnership between Africa/AU and India, compared to other emerging actors actively involved in the continent.

Endnotes

1   India - African Union Relations, http://www.mea.gov.in/Portal/ForeignRelation/
    india-african-union-relations-march-2012.pdf

2   Ibid.

3   Address by Vice President at the 50th Anniversary Summit of OAU/AU in Addis
    Ababa May 25, 2013, http://www.mea.gov.in/in-focus article.htm?21747/Addr
    ess+by+Vice+President+at+the+50th+Anniversary+Summit+of+OAUAU+in+A
    ddis+Ababa

4   India - African Union Relations, http://www.mea.gov.in/Portal/ForeignRelation/
    india-african-union-relations-march-2012.pdf

5   Ibid.

6   Ibid.

7   Ibid.

8   Ibid.

9   Ibid.

10 Ibid.

11 Ibid.

12 Vinay Kumar, Joint Secretary, MEA, Government of India, http://
    diplomacyandforeignaffairs.com/vinay-kumar-joint-secretary-mea-government-
    of-india/

13 Ibid.

14 Ibid.

15 Ibid.

16 NetIndian News Network, November 19, 2010, http://netindian.in/
    news/2010/11/19/0008743/india-holds-meeting-african-regional-economic-
    communities

17 2nd India-RECs Meeting, November 09, 2011, http://mea.gov.in/press-releases.
    htm?dtl/7316/Second+IndiaRECs+Meeting

18 3rd India- Regional Economic Communities (RECs) Meeting August 20, 2014, http://www.mea.gov.in/press-releases.htm?dtl/23943/3rd+India+Regional+Economic+Communities+RECs+Meeting

19 Sandipani Dash, "India's Partnership with RECs in Africa,"http://www.icwa.in/pdfs/VP/2014/PartnershipwithRECinAfrica.pdf

20 Ashutosh Varshney, "India's Democratic Challenge", *Foreign Affairs,* March-April 2007, http://www.foreignaffairs.com/articles/62451/ashutosh-varshney/indias-democratic-challenge

21 UNDP, India Election Diary 2014: Namibia's Electoral Team Studies the Elections, http://www.in.undp.org/content/india/en/home/ourwork/democraticgovernance/successstories/india-election-diary-2014--namibias-electoral-team.html

22 UNDP, http://eci.nic.in/ECI_Main/CI_2013/TEsUNDP_07032014.pdf

23 Ibid.

24 MEA, India-Sudan Relations, http://www.mea.gov.in/Portal/ForeignRelation/Sudan_July_2014__2_.pdf

25 Second Africa-India Forum Summit 2011: Africa-India Framework for Enhanced Cooperation, May 25, 2011, http://mea.gov.in/bilateral-documents.htm?dtl/34/Second+AfricaIndia+Forum+Summit+2011+AfricaIndia+Framework+for+Enhanced+Cooperation

26 MEA, India-Egypt Relations, http://www.mea.gov.in/Portal/ForeignRelation/Egypt_July_2014.pdf

27 MEA, India-Libya Relations, http://www.mea.gov.in/Portal/ForeignRelation/Libya_-_July_2014.pdf

28 MEA, India-Mauritus Relations,http://www.mea.gov.in/Portal/ForeignRelation/Mauritus_July_2014__.pdf

29 MEA, India- Tunisia Relations, http://www.mea.gov.in/Portal/ForeignRelation/Tunisia_July_2014.pdf

30 Election Commission of India, Press Note, 21 September 2011, Nigerian Election Commissioners Begin Study Visit to India International Institute of Democracy And Election Management, http://eci.nic.in/eci_main1/current/PN21092011.pdf

31 MEA, India-Nigeria Relations, http://www.mea.gov.in/Portal/ForeignRelation/Nigeria_Aug_2014.pdf

32 Election Commission of India, Press Note, http://eci.nic.in/eci_main1/current/pn_iidem.pdf

33 Ibid.

34 Indian Express, November 4, 2014, "Polls Apart", http://indianexpress.com/article/opinion/columns/polls-apart-3/99/

35 Address by Vice President at the 50th Anniversary Summit of OAU/AU in Addis Ababa, May 25, 2013, http://www.mea.gov.in/in-focus-article.htm?21747/Address+by+Vice+President+at+the+50th+Anniversary+Summit+of+OAUAU+in+Addis+Ababa

Chapter - 7

African Unity: AU's Appraisal

The multiplicity of wars and armed conflicts in Africa, coupled with diverse security threats and challenges, has refocused international policy and academic attention on the peace- security development nexus. A particular area of concern is what role African regional economic and security organisations can play in conflict stabilisation, conflict management and winning the peace in transition societies in post-Cold War Africa. Here is an attempt made to critically explore the nexus of peace, security and development within the framework of the resurgence of economic and security regionalisms with a particular focus on regionalist projects in Africa, including ECOWAS in West Africa, SADC in Southern Africa and IGAD in the Horn of Africa.[1] These sub-regional groupings are operating under the overarchic institutional direction of the African Union (AU). It is, therefore, necessary to explore the role of viable, strong and modern states in driving and strengthening the nexus within the framework of economic and security regionalism in Africa.

This chapter has summed up the findings of the above chapters and has found out an overall understanding of the AU's interrelationship with the state system, existing and emerging social fault lines, and the multiple regionalisms in Africa. It has also tried to explore the contours, constraints and capacity of the interface among the AU leadership, its member countries and the emerging extra-regional powers.

Redefining Peace, Security and Developmental Regionalism

Nowhere in the world are the problems and challenges of security and development more prominent than in Africa. The multiplicity of wars, armed conflicts and security threats (from both military and non-military sources) has foisted on academics, policy practitioners and development and conflict interveners the imperative to engage with the link between peace, security and development (henceforth the 'nexus'). A focus on economic and security integration in Africa provides an innovative perspective and context for understanding the connections of the nexus. The inextricable link between economic regionalism and security integration highlights the fact that it is impossible to achieve the economic growth and development objectives of integration in an environment of wars, armed conflicts and perpetual regional political instability. Violent wars and multiple security threats have challenged the narrow traditional academic and policy approaches to Development Studies, Peace Studies and Security Studies as separate disciplines with little or no interconnectedness.[2]

Africa provides a range of challenges and opportunities for understanding the conceptual, policy-relevant and empirical understanding of the nexus. To illustrate the critical connections, this is to advance the framework of a peace-security development nexus as a disciplinary bridge for understanding this nexus. It is necessary to outline the international policy setting, which leads to an interpretation of peace and security theoretically linked to developmental regionalism and cast in terms of new regionalism in Africa. There is a need to apply the concept and practice of the peace security-development nexus to European Union integration, assessing insights and applicability for Africa.[3]

It is pertinent to examine as to how wars and armed conflicts have undermined the achievement of the regional economic integration and development objectives, and in the process forced on the regionalist projects the imperative to develop peace, security and conflict management mechanisms as a strategy to maintain regional peace and security – the prerequisite for regional economic growth and development. There is also an urgency to evaluate regional case studies: regional economic integration and peacekeeping interventions in West Africa; regional economic and developmental regionalism in the Horn of Africa; and regional economic and security integration in Southern Africa. It is argued that despite the limitations and challenges facing Africa's economic and security regionalisms, especially the fact that weak states drive the regionalisation process, the continent provides valuable insight into understanding not only the dynamics of the peace-security-development nexus, but also how to strengthen the policy approaches and responses to development and conflict interventions.[4]

Security and Development Agenda Setting

A glance at the literature and policy practice of conflict and development interventions by a range of national, regional and international actors illustrates that regional economic and security integration has been the missing link in development and security studies. These actors have assumed a positive correlation between security and development. This assumption has recently been applied to the practice of economic and security regionalism in Africa with the understanding that conflict can no longer be treated primarily as a peace and security issue, but rather should be treated as an important development issue. This raises some questions. How do we know that there is a positive correlation between security and development? How do we theoretically and methodologically explain this correlation?

Evidence suggests that the assumed positive correlation is not rooted in rigorous research and in-depth policy analysis. The policies and social realities of the security-development nexus are disjointed and do not provide a coherent and useful guide for conflict and development interventions. In effect this nexus has been policy-driven and not research driven.

In addition, the compartmentalisation of security and development as separate disciplines has obfuscated the critical connections. To understand the disciplinary intersections, one should start by challenging some of the dominant discourses on development and security, in particular the imposition of 'security', 'development' and 'liberal peace' agendas on the developing world. A research programme should also include an evaluation of the effects of the policies and interventions of the rich countries (the global North) on developing countries (the global South). In addition, there is need to focus on human development and security that confronts both vertical and horizontal inequalities, in particular the focus on the resilience of developing countries and peoples. A critical dimension is how to engage with the failure of development in the South and why does the international community "conveniently" ignore some of the failures? Rather than simply describe the security-development nexus in terms of positive outcomes, we should recognise and incorporate the tensions, contradictions and potential social costs in the implementation of the nexus.

This requires a critical review of the informal dimensions of 'development' (e.g. informal economy) and 'security' (e.g. civil militias), and how to utilise local and regional actors in conflict and development interventions owned by the local communities and peoples. Security and development are thus mutually reinforcing, though with tensions, contradictions and potential social costs. Let us now endeavour to provide an understanding of the narrow and traditional compartmentalisation of development, security and peace studies, and try to reconceptualise them...Rather than simply describe the security development nexus in terms of positive outcomes, we should recognise and incorporate the tensions, contradictions and potential social costs in the implementation of the nexus.[5]

Traditionally, economic integration has been treated as an approach to regional economic growth and development, creating concepts such as customs union theory, transactionalism, functionalism and neo-functionalism to explain the phenomenon of international integration.[6] Even within the disciplines of Political Science and International Relations, despite acknowledging the normative underpinnings of regional economic integration as an approach to peace and security, not much effort was made conceptually and empirically to explore the connections between regional economic integration, peace and security – in particular how they reinforce each other. More recently the political economy approach to regional economic integration, cast in terms of the new regionalism debate within the context of globalisation, has contributed to bringing the academic and policy debate on the nexus between peace, security and economic regionalism to the fore. To understand the linkages it is important to start with brief definitions for peace, security, development and economic integration.

Defining Peace

If we argue that there may be a link between peace, security and development, it is important to illustrate what kind of peace are we referring to, specifically peace for 'whom' and for 'what purpose'. Peace is a contested concept and has attracted different interpretations. Briefly peace is about the absence of war, fear, conflict, anxiety, human suffering and violence and about peaceful co-existence. The Norwegian peace theorist, Johann Galtung has pointed to three types of violence relevant to the understanding of peace: direct violence (physical, emotional and psychological); structural violence (i.e. deliberate policies and structures that cause human suffering, death and harm); and cultural violence (i.e. cultural norms and practices that create discrimination, injustice and human suffering).[7] Galtung also differentiates between 'negative peace' – the absence of direct violence, war, fear and conflict at individual, national, regional and international levels – and 'positive peace': the absence of unjust structures, unequal relationships and injustice, and inner peace at an individual level.

While these conceptual categories may be useful, it is important to highlight that different cultures and civilisations have different interpretations of peace which are grounded in the particular historical experience and specific political context of a country, society or region. For example, the majority of people in the Great Lakes region of Africa associate peace with the absence of war and armed conflict, while those in Southern Africa associate peace with the absence of depressing social and development indicators such as poverty and the AIDS pandemic.[8] The concept of peace in all its manifestations is therefore about security, development and social justice. It is this broader understanding of peace that links it to security and development.

Redefining Security

A reconceptualisation of peace, conflict and development practice illustrates the inextricable link between peace and security. According to Terry Terriff et al (1999), even though peace is widely accepted as the absence of warfare, the concept of peace has remained unexplored, until recently, as a security issue.[9] But how do we define security and how does it relate to peace? Security, albeit a 'contested concept', is generally understood to be about the condition of feeling safe from harm or danger, the defence, protection and preservation of core values and the absence of threats to acquired values. Put simply, security is about survival and the conditions of human existence.[10] The traditional concept of security has largely focused on the threat and use of force. This largely military conception of security has focused on the state as the primary referent object of security.

Various scholars have criticised the traditional military conception of security because it does not account for the emerging non-military sources of threat to security at the individual, societal, state, regional and global levels. This has led to the broadening of the concept to embrace non-military dimensions such as environment, migration, ethno-religious and nationalist identities, poverty and economic insecurity, and disease. This broadening of the security agenda is now described as Critical Security Studies. In the African context there are both military and non-military sources of security threat. Security is about protection and preservation from fear and danger that threatens the survival of societies and peoples. It is about survival and the conditions of human existence in a continent with depressing social and development indicators, with an estimated 47 per cent of the population in sub-Saharan Africa living on less than a dollar a day. Security, therefore, is about peace, development and justice because the absence of all three of these creates the conditions for conflict and armed violence. In this conceptualisation we see the inextricable linkages between peace and security and the imperative for the securitisation of peace.

Securitising Development

Violent wars in Africa and the devastating consequences on development and security highlight the limitations of the traditional interpretation of development studies and practice. The emerging post-Cold War debate is on the securitisation of development, i.e. treating development as a security issue because wars and armed conflicts exacerbate the problems of underdevelopment and insecurity. The problems of underdevelopment such as poverty, social exclusion and gross violations of human rights in some cases instigate violent conflicts. Hence development studies and practice have been forced to look beyond their traditional focus to critical issues such as peace, security and the impact of violent conflict. But what is development and what type of development are we describing, in particular development by and for whom and for what purpose? Some argue that development is a relative term, meaning different things to different peoples and communities.

In general, the concept is a positive one, connoting 'progress' or 'change for the better'. As such the definition has embraced: economic growth; basic human needs and human development (food, shelter, clothing, education and health care, and freedom, democratic participation and human dignity); sustainable development and political development.[11] From this expanded definition it follows that development is about equality and social justice; positive change at personal, societal, national and global levels; and about peace and security. But development is also driven by contradictions and tensions because the process of achieving positive social change also includes negative social costs.

In the practice of development a whole range of actors – governments, donor agencies, international development and financial institutions and regional groupings – has been silent about the social and destructive costs of development. Furthermore, the dominant development paradigms advanced by the North, such as modernisation and neo-liberalism within the context of globalisation, have emerged as the universal blueprint for the policies and practice of development, and in the process neglected all other alternative forms and approaches to development. Accepting the varied interpretations of development, it becomes easy to appreciate the interconnectedness between peace, security and development. Security is about protection and preservation from fear and danger that threatens the survival of societies and peoples.

Conceptualising Developmental Regionalism

To appreciate the critical connections of the nexus, we have to explore further their links to regional economic integration. The driving force for the establishment of regional economic integration in contemporary world politics has generally been seen as an approach to economic growth and development for maintaining regional peace and security. In economics and development terms, the advantages derived from regional complementarity of goods and services, economies of scale, comparative advantage and industrialisation were motivating factors for the creation of regionalist projects in different parts of the world. Regional political, security and identity-based issues were also reasons motivating geographically proximate states to cooperate and integrate their economies and communities. A dominant interpretation of regional economic integration has to do with the normative assumptions, i.e. about development, regional order, security and peace. In effect regional integration was perceived as a 'good thing'. After World War II international integration became a dominant strategy for international cooperation and regional development.

Functionalists such as David Mitrany argued that the provision of common needs through functional strategies across national borders would unite people and the evolving mutual interactions and interconnectedness would potentially create an identity of community citizenship.[12] Karl Deutsch also outlined a framework for the emergence of a security community that avoided the use of force in inter-state relations and peaceful resolution of conflicts.[13] Both Mitrany and Deutsch, in describing the normative underpinnings of international integration, talked about the potential for developing 'islands of peace' and a 'working peace system' based on liberal economics and democratic politics. However, the normative assumptions are silent on the potentially negative dimensions of regional economic integration, i.e. that increased regional integration has a tendency to create regional conflicts and perpetuate economic exploitation.

Often regional integration carries the risk of reproducing dominant forms of power; the stronger and more developed states tend to be the net beneficiaries.[14] In addition, regional economic integration creates a 'growth pole' detrimental to weaker states in the integration grouping, whereby the majority of the foreign direct investors and regional institutions tend to favour the more developed and stronger states.[15] Finally, regional integration entails a 'pooling of sovereignties' which by implication undermines the political, economic and fiscal sovereignty of member states in a regionalist project.

European Experience of Integration

European integration in the post-war period is one of the few successful examples to demonstrate the peace-security-development nexus. Europe, emerging from the devastation of World War II, experimented with the concept and practice of regional integration and cooperation. In the immediate post-war era, the primary consideration was how to prevent inter-state wars in Europe, create a conducive environment for regional peace, order and security and build cooperation among the states and communities that would ensure interdependence. The difficult transition from post-war recovery to development and dealing with Europe's perpetual security problems led to the creation of a regional integration and cooperation grouping. Consequently when the European Coal and Steel Community was created in 1951 and the European Economic Community (EEC) in 1957, they were based on the notion of sharing regional collective resources in development and security terms.

Between 1960 and 2003 the EEC expanded to 25 member states in a European Union (EU), with a common 'European community identity' – a supranational institution in the form of a European Commission with a parliament and a common currency, the Euro. The established EU governmental structure is based on principles of liberal economics and democratic politics.

But Europe as we know it today has not always been stable and economically developed with viable modern states. William Wallace argues that 'West European integration was a product not only of a common culture and history, and of a particular geographical density, but also of a common disaster and predicament: the war and its aftermath, American hegemony and the Soviet threat' (Wallace 1995:201). To respond to these diverse regional problems, Europe implemented constructive development and security programmes and policies such as the European Common Agricultural Policy (CAP), European Free Trade Association (EFTA) and the Lomé Convention outlining the Africa-Caribbean-Pacific economic relations (ACP), a common market with a customs union, political cooperation and a common foreign and security policy. These regional post-war development and security programmes were supported by the U.S.-backed Marshall Plan.[16]

The regional policies and programmes led to the building and intensification of economic, social, political and security interdependence. In addition, European polices on regime and security convergence led to the political stability and democratic success of former military and authoritarian regimes such as Greece, Spain and Portugal and the new member states from the former Soviet bloc and Eastern Europe.

Traditional 'enemies' such as France and Germany are now locked into a partnership involving economics, security, development and politics. Despite the progress in linking security and development in Europe, however, the EU is still plagued by a perpetual amity-enmity divide about the nature of the European project either as a 'partnership of nations' or a 'federal political union'. The rejection of the EU proposed constitution by France and Holland in 2005 reinforces the view that the security-development nexus is not problem-free. What we see emerging in the EU is a deliberate policy and practice to link regional peace security- development in order to build diverse interdependent states and peoples sharing a 'common European identity'. The EU case also illustrates that viable, strong and modern states are crucial to the nexus at both national and regional levels.[17]

African Experience of Integration

To what extent are African states – most of which have weak, failing and cash-strapped economies – able to lend themselves to the difficult and demanding project of linking peace, security and development both at national and regional levels? Are there any successful African examples? Answering these questions requires examining 'why' and 'how' regional economic integration and cooperation in Africa expanded into the domain of regional peace, security and conflict management. Traditional 'enemies' such as France and

Germany are now locked into a partnership involving economics, security, development and politics.

An overview of contemporary violent conflicts and the socio-development situation in Africa gives an insight into the 'why' and the imperative of the nexus. The post-colonial political and security landscape of Africa is littered with inter-state and intra-state wars and armed conflicts. By 2002 there were 18 active wars and armed conflicts in Africa at different levels of intensity or at different stages of transition from war to peace. Most of these wars are being fought in some of the world's poorest countries. Civilians have become the main target and victims in these civil wars, accounting for more than 90 per cent of the casualties.[18]

According to the UNDP Human Development Report 2002, an estimated 3.6 million people were killed in internal warfare in the 1990s and half of all civilian casualties are children, with an estimated 200,000 child soldiers in Africa of the 300,000 worldwide. The number of refugees and internally displaced persons grew by 50 per cent. The civil wars in Somalia, the Democratic Republic of Congo (DRC), Angola, Liberia, Côte d'Ivoire and Sierra Leone have led to state collapse and societal fragmentation. Attempts have been made to negotiate civil war peace settlements, and multinational peacekeeping forces, both regional and from the United Nations, have been deployed. Low-intensity ethno-religious and political conflicts in Nigeria, Zimbabwe, Guinea-Bissau, Mauritania, Sudan and Central Africa Republic continue to undermine peace and stability on the continent.

The cumulative effect of armed conflicts and instability is that they undermine and deter the attainment of regional economic integration and development objectives. Hence a variety of complex domestic, regional and external factors have forced the originally established economic groupings in Africa to expand into the peace and security domain. Experimental regional peace and security initiatives by originally chartered economic groupings, despite their limitations and shortcomings, illustrate the resilience and resurgence of regionalism in Africa – and a tacit recognition that development and economic integration objectives cannot be achieved in an environment of insecurity, wars and armed conflicts. It is necessary, therefore, to explore the specific regional context of the peace development-security nexus in Africa.

Regional Integration in West Africa

Robert Kaplan portrayed the West African sub-region in 1994 as having the potential to become the 'real strategic danger' threatening international peace and security. The sub-region comprises 16 geographically proximate states that have emerged as distinct political and socio-economic entities. Its diverse political history is reflected in the Anglophone, Francophone and Lusophone colonial divide which has often played itself out in the arena of sub-regional politics. In the immediate post-independence period most countries in the region had promising economic development prospects, but a combination of domestic and external forces have turned the sub-region into one of the least developed in the world. The countries are excessively reliant on official development assistance and export economies based on extracting minerals such as diamonds and oil.

Their demographics describe a large and growing youth population, mostly unemployed, lacking in skills and educational opportunities. These depressing social and development indicators have a devastating impact on the sustainability of human security. In the 1990s the combined effects of the end of the Cold War and the negative impacts of globalisation, coupled with the nature of domestic politics and economic decay, led to state collapse and civil wars as in Liberia, Sierra Leone, Guinea Bissau, Mali and Côte d'Ivoire. The nature of conflicts in West Africa demonstrates the importance of understanding the 'regional conflict complex' exacerbated by local, intra-state, regional and international factors. These armed conflicts are not just confined to state borders, but the regional dynamics also often fuel and sustain these wars through the activities of the shadow economy and 'peace spoilers'. The military security threats include criminal and intra-communal violence and involve civil militias and mercenaries and the proliferation of light weapons.

In recognition of the security and development challenges faced by the West African states, in 1975 the countries in the sub-region established a regional integration and cooperation grouping in the form of the Economic Community of West African States (ECOWAS), comprising 16 member states and with market integration and common market objectives. ECOWAS has had limited success in achieving its economic integration and development objectives, notably in facilitating intra-regional trade, regional economic growth and social progress, and has had a negligible impact on the lives of West Africans. Despite its attempts at market integration and facilitating the free movement of the factors of production within the region, physical or regional infrastructural integration is limited.[19]

Developments in the 1990s forced ECOWAS to expand into the peace and security domains. These included the devastating impact of violent civil wars in the region which spilled over into neighbouring countries, the changed international political and security environment with the end of the Cold War, and the perceived international neglect of Africa after the Cold War. This prompted the realisation that violent wars and regional instability undermine and prevent the achievement of regional economic and development objectives.

Nigeria, the sub-regional hegemon, was instrumental in the creation of ECOWAS. With the new conflict and security challenges, Nigeria played a leading role in the formation of the regional peacekeeping and intervention force, ECOWAS Ceasefire Monitoring Group (ECOMOG), which gave it the opportunity to promote and achieve its foreign and security policies. ECOMOG was an ad hoc coalition of 'willing states' deployed in 1990 in Liberia to assist in stabilising and managing the civil war. Its experiments in regional peacekeeping and conflict management/stabilisation in West Africa covered: ECOWAS civil war peace settlements and ECOMOG peacekeeping and conflict management in Liberia from 1990 to 1997, and ECOWAS Mission in Liberia (ECOMIL) in August 2003; ECOWAS/ECOMOG peacekeeping and 'democratic intervention' in Sierra Leone (ECOMOG II) in 1998; ECOWAS as peace broker and ECOMOG ceasefire monitoring in Guinea Bissau in 1999; and ECOWAS civil war peace settlement and ECOMICI conflict stabilisation in Cote d'Ivoire in 2004.

The ECOWAS experiments in maintaining regional peace, security and order have been supported by UN-ECOMOG co-deployment peacekeeping and peace support operations, external pivotal states interventions such as the British 'Operation Palliser' in Sierra Leone, French peacekeeping deployment in Côte d'Ivoire, and U.S. military deployment in Liberia in 2003. The nature of conflicts in West Africa demonstrates the importance of understanding the 'regional conflict complex' exacerbated by local, intra-state, regional and international factors.

In the light of the above, West Africa may not be the best example of linking peace, security and development because the efforts to respond to regional conflict and security challenges have not been based on constructive and long-term strategies to link the issues. In addition member states of ECOWAS, in pursuit of selfish strategic interests, have supported and instigated wars and armed conflicts in neighbouring states. An example is the Liberia backed insurgency in Sierra Leone. Even within the framework of regional peacekeeping intervention the members have often failed to agree on a common foreign and security policy. Furthermore, ECOMOG peacekeeping and intervention efforts have been largely in pursuit of Nigeria's political security and economic and military strategic interests. Regional peacekeepers have been involved in gross violations of human rights and the exploitation of war economies in both Liberia and Sierra Leone. It is therefore questionable whether the ECOWAS expansion into the peace and security domain provides building blocs for promoting the realisation of the nexus.[20]

Regional Integration in the Horn of Africa

In contrast to the West African sub-region, a variety of developmental challenges caused by natural disasters such as drought and famine, further accentuated by perennial wars and violent conflicts, have forced countries in the Horn of Africa to develop policies that illustrate the nexus. The Horn comprises Sudan, Somalia, Djibouti, Ethiopia, Eritrea, Kenya and Uganda. The Horn demonstrates diversity in ecological, political, socio-cultural and economic terms. Most of its peoples depend on subsistence agriculture and pastoralism in the face of scarce natural resources. The pervasiveness of conflict and the rampant use of landmines in the region have had devastating effects on economic activities and the environment. Most countries in the Horn have implemented structural adjustment programmes with varying degrees of success. Their level of development is reflected in depressing economic and social indicators, reinforcing the perception of the region as a 'disaster zone'.

Peter Woodward comments that the Horn is the 'stage on which Africa's tragedy is played out in stark and violent form'.[21] The regional impacts of environmental and development problems on human security led to the formation of the Inter-Governmental Authority on Drought and Development (IGADD) in 1986. IGADD initially focused on issues of drought, famine and desertification in the region. The resurgence of regionalism in world politics in the 1990s caused the political leadership of IGADD to consider transforming the authority, and at an extraordinary summit in Addis Ababa in 1995 the decision was taken to revitalise the institution and to expand its remit to cover peace and security. At a 1996 summit in Nairobi IGADD agreed to establish the Inter-Governmental Authority on Development (IGAD).

Its three primary areas of focus were food security and environmental protection; infrastructural development (transport and communications) and regional conflict prevention, management and resolution; and humanitarian affairs. An evident manifestation of the peace-security-development nexus in the Horn is the shift in IGAD's original preoccupation with environmental protection and development cooperation to, now, a concern with regional peace and security. IGAD has made efforts to facilitate civil war peace settlements in Somalia and Sudan in collaboration with sub-regional pivotal states such as Kenya and Ethiopia, and other external actors such the EU, the U.S. and the African Union.

An evident manifestation of the peace security-development nexus in the Horn is the shift in IGAD's original preoccupation with environmental protection and development cooperation to, now, a concern with regional peace and security. Though the developmental regionalism efforts by IGAD have not provided the expected economic and development benefits, due to a combination of national, regional and international factors, the regional organisation has started to put into place the structures and mechanisms for linking regional peace, security and development. It has established the IGAD Centre for Conflict Early Warning and Response Mechanism and facilitated conflict management in both Sudan and Somalia. The expectation is that peace and stability in the Horn will potentially create a conducive environment for the achievement of regional economic and developmental objectives.[22]

However, it is premature to perceive the peace and security efforts by IGAD as laying a solid foundation for regional security and development. IGAD member states, like ECOWAS countries, habitually intervene to instigate armed conflict in neighbouring countries. IGAD countries have failed to forge a common foreign and security policy necessary for regional peace and a stable political order. Rather, the relative success of IGAD's preventive diplomacy efforts in both Sudan and Somalia has been made possible by the EU-IGAD Partnership Forum and U.S. financial, political and diplomatic backing. In particular the Bush Administration, for a variety of political considerations, including pressures from the American Christian right, the 'war on terror' and oil energy needs, has backed the Sudan and Somalia civil war peace settlements.

Regional Integration in Southern Africa

The heterogeneous regional space now described as 'Southern Africa', according to Fredrick Söderbaum, has been collectively constructed by 'state, market, society and external actors in a historical perspective'.[23] The political history of Southern Africa had been largely dominated by the struggles for political independence of Angola and Mozambique from Portuguese colonial domination, the political liberation of Zimbabwe and Namibia and the struggle against apartheid South Africa and its policy of regional destabilisation. The end of the Cold War ushered in a wave of democratic governance in Southern Africa and led to the transformation of some of its authoritarian and anti-democratic regimes. South Africa is the economic giant in the sub-region. Though Britain, the U.S., Japan and Germany remain South Africa's main trading partners, Southern Africa is emerging as an increasingly strategic and valuable export market.

However, the depressing social and development indicators in Southern Africa not only reveal the disparity between the countries of the region, but also manifest the multidimensional security problems and challenges that belie the putative economic growth and development in the SADC region. Life expectancy at birth in 2001 of relatively developed countries such as Seychelles and Mauritius is 72.2 and 71.6 years respectively. This is in sharp contrast with life expectancy in other relatively developed states in the region such as South Africa (50.9), Namibia (47.4), and Botswana (44.7).[24]The AIDS pandemic is largely responsible for this depressing disparity.

The multiple security and development challenges led to the creation of the Southern African Development Co-ordinating Conference (SADCC) in 1980 as the regional development mechanism to respond to these problems. However, SADCC's sectoral development approach was a failure, and coupled with the changed international security and political environment with the end of the Cold War, the regional body was transformed in 1992 to the Southern African Development Community (SADC) with a common market objective. The end of apartheid in South Africa and of the Cold War have led to relative political stability in much of Southern Africa.

Regional integration in Southern Africa, like West Africa and the Horn, is driven by an 'amity-enmity-dynamic.' While it may foster mutual interdependence and an ethos of collective security, it may also lead to competition, conflict, mutual suspicion and a lack of peaceful co-existence.

The personality conflict between former President Nelson Mandela of South Africa and President Robert Mugabe of Zimbabwe flowed into the complex politics of the region, with South Africa emerging as the reluctant sub-regional hegemon and Zimbabwe as the hegemonic pretender – in effect dividing the region into rival political camps, the 'two SADCs'.

The civil war in the Democratic Republic of Congo and the threat to regional peace and security led to intervention by neighbouring states such as Uganda, Rwanda and Burundi on the one hand, and the deployment of the SADC Allied Armed Forces (SADC-AAF), including Zimbabwe, Namibia and Angola, on the other. This gave rise to what has been described as 'Africa's First World War' and the partitioning of DRC in to rival security, military, economic and political spheres of strategic interests. The deployment of the SADC-AAF peacekeeping and conflict stabilisation force helped to contain the conflict, forced ceasefire and peace agreements on the warring factions, succeeded in stopping some of the killings and created a fragile security situation that ensured the survival of the Kinshasa government. It also made possible the deployment of the French-led EU peacekeeping force – Operation Atermis – in the east of the country. This paved the way for the withdrawal of foreign troops by Rwanda and Uganda and the eventual deployment of a UN peacekeeping mission, MONUC. The peace has yet to hold and is threatened by a variety of regional 'spoiler' problems.

SADC expansion into regional peacekeeping and conflict management, like that of ECOWAS, has been fraught with problems. There is a debate as to whether the SADC intervention was a peacekeeping deployment or a 'coalition of willing states', in particular Zimbabwe, in pursuit of strategic security and economic interests in a 'free-for-all' exploitation of DRC's war economy. This article argues that SADC's expansion into regional conflict management has not been based on a coherent policy approach in linking the nexus in practical terms. Rather, this ad hoc intervention is largely driven by the diverse and conflicting strategic interests of major regional partners. The real challenge for SADC is how to capitalise on this ad hoc intervention to begin the process of institutionalising the linkage.

Institutionalising Security Development Linkage

Returning to the question of Africa's potential to provide constructive examples of the nexus at national and regional levels, the response is both 'no' and 'yes'. While efforts undertaken so far have been fraught with challenges that lead to questions of sustainability, sub-regional examples unfailingly illustrate 'why' and 'how' we need to understand the nexus in Africa. In all the three regional case studies, the lack of pre-existing integrative approaches to development and security led to violent wars and armed conflicts, state collapse, warlordism and societal fragmentation. Now, however, some tentative efforts are being made to tackle problems of violent conflicts and insecurity in an integrative regional manner. The ECOWAS/ECOMOG peacekeeping and conflict management interventions in West Africa have reinforced the need for a stable regional integration in Southern Africa, like West Africa and the Horn, is driven by an amity-enmity dynamic.

Peace, security and political order are required to achieve development and economic growth. Similar lessons could be drawn from the preventive diplomacy interventions of IGAD and the SADC-AAF deployment. Out of these ad hoc, 'fire brigade' interventions we see the emergence of regional mechanisms put in place to attempt to address the peace, conflict, security and development problematic. Examples are the ECOWAS 1999 Protocol Relating to the Mechanism for Conflict Prevention, Management, Resolution, Peacekeeping and Security and the 1996 SADC Organ for Politics, Defence and Security. However, the mere establishment of these regional peace and security structures does not guarantee practical implementation.

Several key lessons from the European model explaining the nexus are relevant for Africa. First, for regional economic and security integration to succeed there should be strong, viable and modern states; this has not been the case in Africa. Any project in Africa linking security and development will require efficient political and economic management of the state. Furthermore the international systemic factors that marginalise African countries in accessing world markets and global economic forces all pose serious external challenges to the possibility of efficient African states and therefore reduce the possibility of successfully linking security and development. Second, the European experience shows that consolidating the gains of the security-development nexus is a drawn-out and gradual process, not a 'quick-fix' project. Some media commentators and international policy practitioners are often critical of Africa's slow pace or lack of progress in establishing the nexus in practical terms; hence we see depictions of Africa as the 'Hopeless Continent', as The Economist described it in 2000. These analysts do not take into account that it has taken Europe more than six decades to successfully link regional peace, security and development.[25]

Despite available EU lessons, African sub-regional economic and security integration experiments have not yet produced a viable model for Africa. A variety of reasons account for this, including the nature of domestic politics and bad governance leading to armed conflicts and state collapse. Most of the states in Africa are weak and therefore do not have the capacity to lend themselves to the demanding tasks of linking regional peace, security and development. Three decades on, regional economic and security integration in Africa is still driven by the governing elites with limited participation by civil society and, worse still, lack of societal ownership of the regionalisation process. In addition Africa's regionalist projects are far too busy copying EU and OSCE (the Organisation for Security and Cooperation in Europe) models of economic and security integration, rather than exploring alternative strategies of linking the nexus that are context-specific and historically relevant and reflect the African realisms.

It is clear that opportunities exist in Africa to link peace, development and security, as witnessed by the nascent institutional mechanisms and ad hoc structures being established in all the regional examples. The real challenge is how to move beyond the ad hoc approach to long-term regional strategies of institutionalising the nexus. Perhaps the international political commitment and goodwill generated by the 'Year of Africa' (2005) provides a window of opportunity to incorporate the nexus into all international policy processes and responses on Africa. Rather than conclude on a pessimistic note, it is clear that opportunities exist in Africa to link peace, development and security, as witnessed by the nascent institutional mechanisms and ad hoc structures being established in all the regional examples.

Financial In/dependence

The AU's Peace and Security Protocol (PSC) Protocol, article 21, established the Peace Fund to provide "financial resources for peace support missions and other operational activities related to peace and security". The Protocol requires the Fund to be made up of financial appropriations from the regular AU budget; voluntary contributions from Member States, international partners and other sources, such as the private sector, civil society and individuals; as well as through fund-raising activities. The Chairperson of the AU Commission is mandated to raise and accept voluntary contributions from sources outside Africa, in conformity with the AU's objectives and principles. The Peace Fund is operational and receives funds for all Peace and Security Department activities.[26]

The PSC Protocol also envisaged a revolving trust fund within the broader Peace Fund that would provide a standing reserve for specific projects in case of emergencies and unforeseen priorities. The level of funding required in the revolving trust fund is to be determined by the relevant AU policy organs on recommendation by the PSC. In order to meet the costs of the AU's peace and security commitments, AU Heads of State and Government decided in January 2010 to increase Member States' assessed contributions from six per cent to 12 per cent within three years, starting in 2011 (EX.CL/Dec.524(XVI)). However, because of a shortage of funds, the current (as of August 2014) rate of contribution by Member States is seven percent. AU peace and security activities also receive significant support from international partners.[27]

The AU has indeed demonstrated excessive dependence of its operation on external financial support. Its 80 per cent of funding is received from external sources, such as the EU, World Bank, IMF and AfDB, while rest 20 per cent is mobilised from member countries. A significant proportion (around 75 per cent) of internal funding was being contributed by only five member countries, namely South Africa, Nigeria, Libya, Egypt and Algeria. The proportion of internal funding has gone down following political and security unrest in Libya and Egypt in recent years. On peace and security front, the proportion of AU's external funding is as much as 90 per cent, with funds coming from countries like Denmark, the Netherlands, Norway, Sweden, France and China.[28]

The High-Level Panel on Alternative Sources of Funding the AU led by the former Nigerian President, Olusegun Obasanjo and composed of Edem Kodjo, former Secretary General of the OAU and Luisa Diogo, former Prime Minister and Minister of Finance of Mozambique, presented its report at the 21st Ordinary Session of the AU's Assembly, a session which also marked the 50th anniversary of the establishment of the OAU/AU. After consideration of various proposals, the Assembly adopted the Report in principle as well as the two options proposed as alternative sources of financing the AU: a) US$ 2.00 hospitality levy per stay in a hotel; and b) US$ 10.00 levy on flight tickets for flights originating from Africa or with destinations in Africa.[29]

Article 19 of the AU Constitutive Act provides for three specific financial organs to be created, the African Central Bank (ACB), African Investment Bank (AIB) and African Monetary Fund (AMF). The role of these institutions is to implement the economic integration called for in the 1991 Treaty Establishing the African Economic Community (Abuja Treaty). The 1999 Sirte Declaration, under which the OAU decided to create the AU, called for the speedy establishment of all institutions proposed in the Abuja Treaty.[30]

The AU Assembly has adopted protocols for the establishment of the AIB and AMF (detailed as follows). The draft Protocol for the Establishment of the ACB has not yet been submitted to the Assembly. Proposed structures will be submitted to the Executive Council for approval once the protocols for each institution come into force. The ACB's purpose will be to build a common monetary policy and single African currency as a way to accelerate economic integration as envisaged in articles 6 and 44 of the Abuja Treaty. The ACB's objectives will be to: promote international monetary cooperation through a permanent institution, promote exchange stability and avoid competitive exchange rates depreciation, assist in the establishment of a multilateral system of payments in respect of current transactions between members and eliminate foreign exchange restrictions that hamper the growth of world trade. It is proposed that the ACB Headquarters will be in Abuja, Nigeria.[31]

The AIB's purpose will be to foster economic growth and accelerate economic integration in Africa, as envisaged by articles 6 and 44 of the Abuja Treaty. The AIB's objectives will be to: promote public and private sector investment activities intended to advance AU member state regional integration, utilise available resources for the implementation of investment projects contributing to strengthening of the private sector and modernisation of rural sector activities and infrastructures, mobilise resources from capital markets inside and outside Africa for the financing of investment projects in African countries and provide technical assistance as may be needed in African countries for the study, preparation, financing and execution of investment projects. The AIB will be located in Libya.[32] The AU Assembly established the AIB at its February 2009 Summit with the adoption of the Protocol and Statute on the African Investment Bank.[33] The Protocol and Statute will enter into force 30 days after ratification by 15 Member States.

As of 1 September 2014, 20 Member States had signed and two had ratified the Protocol establishing the AIB.[34]

The AMF's purpose will be to facilitate the integration of African economies by eliminating trade restrictions and providing greater monetary integration, as envisaged under articles 6 and 44 of the Abuja Treaty. The Fund is expected to serve as a pool for central bank reserves and AU Member States' national currencies. The Fund will prioritise regional macro-economic objectives in its lending policies. The specific AMF objectives include: a) providing financial assistance to AU member states, b) acting as a clearing house as well as undertaking macro-economic surveillance within the continent, c) coordinating the monetary policies of Member States and promoting cooperation between their monetary authorities, d) encouraging capital movements between member states. The Headquarters of the AMF will be in Yaoundé, Cameroon.[35] The AU Assembly established the AMF at the Malabo Summit in June 2014 with the adoption of the Protocol and Statute for the Establishment of the African Monetary Fund.[36] The Protocol and Statute will enter into force 30 days after ratification by 15 member states. As at 1 September 2014, no Member States had signed or ratified the Protocol.[37]

The Heads of State And Government of the AU made a commitment in 2015 to finance 25 per cent of the cost of AU peace support operations. At the 27th AU Summit held in Rwandan capital Kigali in July 2016, the AU's Assembly decided to operationalize the Peace Fund, in order to finance AU's peace and security operations. The Peace Fund is expected to gain $65 million per year from each of the continent's five regions through an import levy of 0.2 per cent on eligible imports. The provision would increase to $80 million per region by 2020. The funding would be used to support the AU's five peace and security programmes: African Stand by Force (ASF), Panel of the Wise (PoW), Continental Early Warning Systems (CEWS), Capacity Building and Conflict Prevention. [38]

United Nations Secretary-General Ban Ki-moon welcomed the decision by the Assembly of Heads of State and Government of the AU. The Secretary-General's spokesperson issued a statement in this context:

> He notes with interest the innovative funding arrangements aimed at providing the AU, via the Peace Fund, with increased financial means to address the peace and security challenges facing the continent..... Mindful

that a strong partnership requires strong partners, the Secretary-General looks forward to the implementation of this additional step towards the further consolidation of the United Nations-AU partnership.[39]

As per the funding model, every member country would contribute 0.2 percent of its eligible imports (excludes imports exclude products such as medicines, fertilizers and baby food) to the AU. The new model, which would raise about $1.2 billion each year – triple the current AU's annual administrative budget, would be more efficient than the current method, in which most of the funds came from foreign donor countries. The contributions will officially start in 2017. The money would be collected by local revenue authorities and held in central bank accounts, from which the cash would be automatically disbursed. In the existing model, African countries only contribute 28 percent of the AU budget. The rest of the money is donated by the United Nations and western donors to fund humanitarian and peacekeeping operations. The AU's introduction of this new funding model would ensure the continental body become self-reliant and less dependent on foreign donors to run its affairs and finance peace keeping missions across the region.[40]

The AU has thus moved towards self-reliance, particularly in relation to the regional body's peace and security budget. The AU has accordingly evolved as a Pan-African entity with its mandate for 'comprehensive security' in the continent, implying its pursuit of three security objectives: resolution of armed conflicts, political stability and economic security.

Endnotes

1   David J. Francis (2006), "Linking Peace, Security and Developmental Regionalism: Regional Economic and Security Integration in Africa," *Journal of Peacebuilding & Development*, 2 (3), p.7

2   Ibid, p.8.

3   Ibid.

4   Ibid.

5   Ibid, p.9

6   J. Caporaso, 1998, "Regional Integration Theory: Understanding Our Past and Anticipating Our Future," *Journal of European Public Policy*, 5 (1), pp. 1-16; R. Keohane & J. Nye Jr, 1987, "Power and Interdependence Revisited", *International Organization*, Fall.

7   Johann Galtung, 1996, *Peace by Peaceful Means: Peace and Conflict, Development and Civilisation*, London: Sage

8   F. Freedman & N. Poku, 2005, "The Socio-Economic Context of HIV/AIDS", *Review of International Studies*, 31 (4), pp. 665-686.

9   T. Terriff, S. Croft, L. James & P. Morgan, 1999, *Security Studies Today*, Cambridge: Polity.

10   B. Buzan, 1991, *People, States and Fear*, London: Longman; T. Thomas, & P. Wilkin, 1999 eds, *Globalisation, Human Security and the African Experience*, Boulder: Lynne Rienner.

11   T. Allen & A. Thomas, 2000, eds, *Poverty and Development in the 21st Century*, Oxford: OUP; P. Burnell & V. Randall, 2005, eds, *Politics in the Developing World*, Oxford: OUP.

12   David Mitrany, 1966, *A Working Peace System*, Chicago: Quadrangle Books.

13   Karl Deutsch, 1957, *Political Community and the North Atlantic Area*, Princeton: Princeton University Press.

14   D. Francis, 2001, *The Politics of Economic Regionalism: Sierra Leone in ECOWAS*, Aldershot: Ashgate; Schulz et al 2001

15 M. Schulz, F. Soderbaum, & J. Ojendal, 2001 eds, *Regionalisation in a Globalising World: A Comparative Perspective on Proms, Actors & Processes*, London: Zed, pp. 1-7 ; Fawcett & Hurrel 1995; Francis 2001.

16 David J. Francis, 2006, p. 12.

17 Ibid, p.13.

18 UNDP (United Nations Development Programme) 2002, Human Development Report 2002: *Deepening Democracy in a Fragmented World*, Oxford: OUP, p.16.

19 David J. Francis, 2006, p. 14.

20 Ibid, p.15.

21 Peter Woodward (2003), *The Horn of Africa: Politics and International Relations*, London: I. B. Tauris, p. 173.

22 David J. Francis, 2006, p. 16.

23 Fredrick Söderbaum (2002), 'The Political Economy of Regionalism in Southern Africa', PhD thesis, Department of Peace and Development Research, Goteborg University, p. 59.

24 UNDP 2004, pp. 238-9.

25 David J. Francis, 2006, p.18.

26 Alhaji Sarjoh Bah, Elizabeth Choge-Nyangoro,Solomon Dersso, Brenda Mofya and Tim Murithi (2014), "African Peace and Security Architecture: A Handbook," Addis Ababa: Friedrich-Ebert-Stiftung (FES)/AU, p.59.

27 Ibid.

28 This is based on findings of the author's field study in Addis Ababa, AU Headquarters, in December 2014.

29 African Union, Economic Affairs Department, July 2013, Modalities of Implementation of the Two Options retained by the Assembly of Heads of State and Government of the African Union on Alternative Sources of Financing the African Union, ea.au.int/en/sites/default/files/Alternative%20Sources%20_E.pdf

30 Alhaji Sarjoh Bah, et al, 2014, p. 100.

31 Ibid.

32 See Assembly/AU/Dec.64(IV).

33 See Assembly/AU/Dec.251(XIII).

34 Alhaji Sarjoh Bah, et al, 2014, p. 100.

35 See EX.CL/Dec.329 (X).

36 See Assembly/ AU/Dec.517(XXIII).

37 Alhaji Sarjoh Bah, et al, 2014, p. 101.

38 UN News Centre, July 2016, "Ban welcomes African Union's fund for peace and security operations on the continent", http://www.un.org/apps/news/story.asp?NewsID=54494#.V5djYJUkqUk

39 Ibid.

40 Kevin Mwanza, "African Union Introduces New Funding Model To Increase Self-Reliance", *AFKInsider*, July 19, 2016 http://afkinsider.com/129882/african-union-introduces-new-funding-model-increase-self-reliance/#sthash.70TztWHT.dpuf

Index